PRAISE FOR *Money Secrets of the Amish*

"Packed with practical, simple, and smart money saving ideas and teeming with great insight into the sensible Amish ways, *Money Secrets of the Amish* will entertain you with stories and retrain your brain to be the savvy money saver you always dreamed you could be."

—BETH WISEMAN, best-selling author of *Plain Promise* and *Seek Me With All Your Heart*

"Sometimes touching, sometimes humorous, and always helpful, author Lorilee Craker pulls us into the family rooms of the Amish and shows us how they make ends meet. Story after story illustrates savvy money management: trading for goods and services, shopping for bargains, living with less, avoiding debt, curbing the desire to impress others. And Craker's journalistic bent provides plenty of takeaway value for the non-Amish. A very worthwhile read whether your bank account is bursting or busting."

—SUZANNE WOODS FISHER, author of *Amish Peace: Simple Wisdom for a Complicated World* and *Lancaster County Secrets*

"America's gone from the #1 creditor nation to one of the top debtor nations in my lifetime, and as a result, our culture and economy has suffered greatly. We need to get back to basics, and Lorilee Craker's informative yet charming book takes us into the Amish microcosm for answers on becoming solvent and fiscally strong once again. Everyone should take a course in Amish frugality before graduation, but since there isn't one, Craker's book fits the bill."

—JAMES "JY" YOUNG, guitarist, singer and songwriter, co-founder of the rock band Styx

"This book i⟦...⟧ded with Mason jars full of Plain ⟦...⟧cy' gal Lorilee Craker rolls up her s⟦...⟧e-by-one, figuring out

how to fit Amish principles to a non-Amish life. She succeeds, and so can you—read *Money Secrets of the Amish* and add weight to your wallet."

—ERIK WESNER, Amishamerica.com; author of *Success Made Simple:*
An Inside Look at Why Amish Businesses Thrive

"Lorilee inspires and impacts your everyday life with this marvelous little read. From buttons to bakery you suddenly realize this conversation is not about just pinching a few pennies but about transforming how we view our everyday lives. I applaud Lorilee for asking the hard questions and pressing in to find honest answers. Forget the mall, kick back, and soak up the delicious wisdom of a life well lived. Thank you, Lorilee, for shaping my everyday!"

—TRACEY BIANCHI, author of *Green Mama*

"*Money Secrets of the Amish* is a practical, doable guide, and it's such fun to read. Lorilee's voice is as engaging and lively as ever, and the wisdom she shares from the Amish community is both inspiring and instructive. I just finished the last page, and my mind is buzzing with all sorts of ways to waste less, want less, and spend less."

—SHAUNA NIEQUIST, author of *Cold Tangerines* and *Bittersweet*

"*Money Secrets of the Amish* isn't so much about making money; it's about family, discipline, and redefining what *wealthy* means. This is a great read that helps us all to see more clearly what's really valuable in our lives."

—JEFF MCMAHON, award-nominated musician and national director/
runner with the Team McGraw endurance program

MONEY SECRETS

❈ OF THE ❈

AMISH

Finding True Abundance in Simplicity,
Sharing, and Saving

LORILEE CRAKER

THOMAS NELSON
Since 1798

NASHVILLE   DALLAS   MEXICO CITY   RIO DE JANEIRO

Published in Nashville, Tennessee, by Thomas Nelson. Thomas Nelson is a trademark of Thomas Nelson, Inc.

Thomas Nelson, Inc., titles may be purchased in bulk for educational, business, fundraising, or sales promotional use. For information, please e-mail SpecialMarkets@ ThomasNelson.com.

This book is intended to provide accurate information with regard to the subject matter covered. However, the Author and the Publisher accept no responsibility for inaccuracies or omissions, and the Author and Publisher specifically disclaim any liability, loss or risk, whether personal, financial, or otherwise, that is incurred as a consequence, directly or indirectly, from the use and/or application of any of the contents of this book.

Permission was granted by friends from the Amish community for use of their insights from interviews for *Money Secrets of the Amish*. Some names have been changed.

Library of Congress Cataloging-in-Publication Data

Craker, Lorilee.
  Money secrets of the Amish : finding true abundance in simplicity, sharing, and saving / Lorilee Craker.
      p. cm.
  Includes bibliographical references and index.
  ISBN 978-1-59555-341-6 (alk. paper)
  1. Consumer education—United States. 2. Thriftiness—United States. 3. Finance, Personal—United States. 4. Amish—United States. I. Title.
  TX336.C73 2011
  640.73—dc22
                                                          2010045825

Printed in the United States of America

11 12 13 14 15 16 RRD 6 5 4 3 2 1

To the memory of my beloved grandma, Elizabeth Brandt Loewen. Visiting the Amish was a portal to your delicious-smelling farm kitchen, your gentle spirit, and your love, which I carry with me always.

❈ ❈ ❈

CONTENTS

✖ ✖ ✖

INTRODUCTION

What possessed me to tell the Amish buggy driver that I was Mennonite on that vacation day in Lancaster County?

After all, I didn't look the part, with my sleeveless, above-the-knee sundress, bright coral nails, jewelry, and makeup. I looked about as Amish as a contestant from *Dancing with the Stars*.

Maybe it was because the Amishman's name was Menno, the same as our mutual fearless leader, Menno Simons, who founded the Mennonite Church in 1525. (He was a Dutch priest who radically upended the spiritual traditions of his day. The Amish would splinter about 170 years later.)

※ ※ ※

Somehow Menno, rocking the bowl haircut, beard, and suspenders, didn't look surprised.

"*Sprechen Sie Deutsch*?" he asked mildly, smiling.

"*Ja, ein klein bisschen*," I said. (How "*klein*"—"little"—I didn't say, but he could probably figure it out when our conversation ran out of steam after a few questions.)

"Well den, *denki* for visiting us," he said, ambling off to cart another buggy-load of "*Englishers*" (anyone not Amish; you could be from Swaziland and they would still call you an *Englisher*) to their destination.

Across time and space, Plain and Fancy, Menno and I had made a connection; both of us were spiritual children of Menno Simons and his revolutionary band of Anabaptists. I marveled that we could still understand each other's language (although Menno might beg to differ), that our cultural cuisine was similar (delectable, carb-based, mostly beige foods, sometimes with a colorful side of chowchow—kind of an Amish kimchi, featuring beans), and that our views of peace and war were in sync.

Another connection: Amish and Mennonites both draw heavily from the Bible for their names. My dad's name was Abram—Abe—and if I had a nickel for every relative named Jake (for Jacob) or Isaac or Lydia, I'd have enough money for a shoofly pie.

So despite my "Fancy" dress and worldly ways, I felt at home with Menno and his ilk, bearded, bonneted (the women, anyway), and covered head to toe in heavy fabric. We had the

※ ※ ※

same point of origin, though the Amish and the Mennonites broke up in 1693, when Jakob Ammann, their founder, got his shorts in a knot about the issue of shunning. (Apparently, the Mennonites weren't as crazy about shunning as he would have liked them to be—he and his followers took their marbles and went somewhere else to play.) Another bee in his bonnet was the matter of buttons. While those sassy Mennonites were binding their shirts and pants with newfangled buttons, Ammann, a tailor by trade, felt strongly that only hook-and-eye fasteners should be used.

Buttons: of the devil. Hook-and-eye fasteners: godly.

I wonder if it made more sense then than it does now?

At any rate, 317 years later, I was buttoning my pants, and Menno was still fastening his.

Despite the "button schism of 1693," and some seriously head-scratching issues of division, I had always felt drawn to the Amish and their gentle, otherworldly ways. A "Thoroughly Modern Millie," somehow I knew there was still a piece of my heritage in Lancaster County, waiting to be found.

THE CRASH

A few months after the economy crashed and Wall Street had driven us all in the ditch money-wise, I was feeling the aftereffects in my own life. The two industries I work for, book publishing and newspaper publishing, were both in a slump, and my work had definitely begun to dry up. My husband had a good job, thankfully, as a computer programmer, and after several months of turbulence and layoffs, it seemed as if he had some semblance of security.

But it was my work as a writer that was supposed to pay for our kids' school tuition and big-ticket items, such as our son's hockey and ice time and plane fare for my widowed mom when she visited us from Winnipeg, a thousand miles away.

Between fewer freelance assignments, pay cuts, and an overall sag in book sales, I was feeling the pinch more and more. How could I continue to pay for everything I needed when the dollars were drying up?

Things stretched tighter when we attempted to move.

What? Were we nuts?

Pretty much so, yes. But after ten years of squeezing into our snug saltbox (and adding two more kids to the one we arrived with), we jumped—yea, lunged—at the chance to snag a bigger house, currently on a "Blue Light Special," super-saver deal just a mile away.

> Call me *ferhoodled* (rough Amish equivalent for "loopy"), but those bonneted, buttonless People were onto something, money-wise.

The only problem was, our snug saltbox was unsalable, literally, having been appraised at twenty-seven thousand dollars less than what we paid for it a decade ago. *Argh.* After freaking out, some tears, gnashing of

✄ ✄ ✄

teeth, and prayers sent up, flare-like, we figured out a way to make it work. But it would mean living with extreme thrift for a while.

Have I mentioned that thrift makes me itch? It totally does.

Menno to the Rescue?

Then one day, I got a dispatch from on high (well, more like a broadcast from public radio, but looking back, it was somewhat epiphanic). NPR was doing a report on how a certain American subculture had managed to emerge, smelling like roses, in a year of utter financial slop. It was the Amish. *My* Amish.

What are Menno and company doing right? I wondered. Because I sure didn't get Menno's memo, and he's not much for Facebook.

I needed to know what was on that memo! So I decided to interview Bill O'Brien, the Lancaster County banker profiled by NPR, the *Wall Street Journal*, Reuters.com, and many other media outlets. I'm a journalist, after all; that's what I do—get to the bottom of things.

Turns out, 95 percent of his clients at HomeTowne Heritage Bank are Amish, and he oversees some $100 million of their loans. Here's the kicker: in 2008, a year of financial doom, when venerable banks had crumpled in hours, Bill's bank had its best year ever.

※ ※ ※

Call me *ferhoodled* (rough Amish equivalent for "loopy"), but those bonneted, buttonless People were onto something, money-wise.

When I investigated, I found out that Amish culture, serene, simple, and rooted in centuries past, held surprising financial wisdom for me. What could I learn from them that would prevent my husband and me from spending our retirement living under a bridge, sucking on bouillon cubes for nourishment? I mean, of course we probably wouldn't, but there's nothing like a global money droop to get the imagination spinning.

In contrast to my paranoia about being overleveraged and underfunded, the Amish were at peace, unruffled, and rich in contentment. As I dug deeper, I realized that these Plain people could teach me a thing or two about money, and what I could do, not only to hold on for dear life during this recession, but to actually thrive.

Dave Ramsey in a Straw Hat

Used to be, I thought "parsimony" was a garnish. I admit, I even had bad dreams in which Dave Ramsey (who looks just like my husband, I've been told a million times) was somehow my accountant and had access to my checkbook and financial records. In these dreams, Ramsey would come at me, leering, with scissors in his hand, threatening to cut my credit cards to smithereens.

※ ※ ※

I'd wake up in a cold sweat, panting, look over at my slumbering husband, and realize something had to give.

During my Period of Extreme Thrift, when I researched the Amish way of wealth, I realized Dave Ramsey wasn't so bad after all. In fact, he's downright Amish in some ways, when it comes to his views on spending and saving. Snap a pair of suspenders on him and the man would fit right in.

At any rate, discovering the money secrets of the Amish gave me and my family a "Total Money Makeover" of a different kind. Beyond tips on saving, spending, and investing, I learned how to live a lifestyle extravagant in peace, sharing, family, and community closeness.

I always thought some of my frugal friends must have a special gift for hunting out savings and bargains, living abundant lives below their means, with money in the bank—a "thrifty bone"—I called it. As I spent time with the Amish and watched and learned their simple money habits, I realized that thrift is more of a muscle,

> Could a clotheshorse, spendthrift, clueless-about-cash girl like me actually spend less, save more, *and* make shoofly pie?

and I intended to work that muscle until it was strong and lean and powerful enough to withstand temptations of all kinds.

But could I pull it off? Could a clotheshorse, spendthrift, clueless-about-cash girl like me actually spend less, save more, *and* make shoofly pie?

❊ ❊ ❊

Yes, yes, and stay tuned—stranger things have happened.

My husband thinks my "Amish money makeover" is a small miracle (wait until I actually bake that pie!). Somehow though, through the course of writing this book, I noticed how the "generous frugality" of these simple people was slowly entering me, influencing me in every dollar I spent.

Wall Street drove all our financial buggies off the road. Can Menno, Moses, and Sadie, et al. help you and me get hitched up and on the right road again?

The answer is a resounding *Ja*!

1

UPSIDE DOWN

Bishop Eli King is a formidable character.

Renowned in Lancaster County as one of the most conservative, by-the-book bishops in the area, Bishop Eli gives off the air of someone who rules a small dictatorship, and not just sixty or so families in his two districts.

For one, he looks just like Abraham Lincoln with his canny-looking, deep-set eyes, prominent chin, and antique beard and clothes. Abe Lincoln with a bowl cut, that is. Rumor has it that Eli will put the *Bann* (excommunication) on you for putting one toe over the Ordnung, the written and unwritten rules of the Amish.

I'm a little scared of him already, and we've only just begun our chat. It doesn't help that I'm perched delicately on the rim of a bathtub, in the middle of a construction site where Eli works.

The only way he would agree to meet with me is if I questioned him during his lunch hour, as he didn't want to take time away from his employer. Coated with carpentry dust, munching an egg salad sandwich, he accepted my thanks for making time during his lunch break. "Being taught to love work makes all the difference," he said, taking another bite. "There's not much spare time when the budget is tight."

The truth is, the budget has been tight for Eli and his People. Even though overall the Amish have hunkered down and weathered the economic hailstorm of the past couple of years much better than the rest of us, they haven't been completely insulated.

According to Amish expert Erik Wesner, author of *Success Made Simple: An Inside Look at Why Amish Businesses Thrive*, the People have felt the decreased demand that comes in a downturn. "A decline in business can trickle down through the community and even affect those businesses that are strictly 'Amish-oriented,'" he said. "So for example, instead of buying a new buggy for your soon-to-be-sixteen-year-old son for a few thousand dollars from the local Amish carriage shop, you might be more inclined to pick one up at the auction for half that."

Adapting to shaky financial times is something the Amish

do extremely well. Instead of buying new buggies, they'll buy used. Jake the Builder will remodel old homes instead of constructing new ones. One Plain housewife I spoke to said that when times are tight, she'll substitute maple syrup (tapped from her own trees, of course) for sugar in her baking and cooking. Wesner tells of a sawmill owner who switched to vegetable oil—acquired free as a throwaway product from local restaurants—to substitute for diesel, amounting to a thousand-dollar monthly savings.

The Amish are resourceful, to be sure, but there's much more to their money success than that.

> "We scrape the bottom of the barrel more than most."
> —Bishop Eli

Why have they managed to do so well, even in the midst of the recession? Eli offered some insights:

"We scrape the bottom of the barrel more than most," Bishop Eli told me, with an Amishman's gift for understatement, and a rather un-Amish, zealous grin.

"When I grew up," he continued, "my parents didn't have more than the necessities. We were taught that when we go away from the plate, it is empty. Today, there is so much wasted food.

"Waste not, want not," he concluded, polishing off the last morsel of his sandwich.

On debt, he had this to say: "Ya gotta make up what you don't have; don't borrow it."

※ ※ ※

On eating out: "We frown upon eating at restaurants." (Many Amish eat out occasionally, but apparently not under Eli's oversight.)

On the Amish work ethic: "We work with our hands so we can help the poor; the Bible says to."

Eli expressed concern about the immoderate spending habits now creeping into Plain life and community. "Money is our biggest danger," he said, stabbing a finger in the air. "Too much leads to foolish spending, fancy foods."

By the time we were ready to wrap up our chat, I felt that Eli had warmed up to me, and I to him. Sure, he's kind of extreme, but I feel that he's a nice man, despite his severe pronouncements.

"I see you're wearing buttons there, Eli," I teased. "I thought buttons were verboten."

He grinned—a wide and blazing grin—and yanked open the top part of his shirt. I nearly fell into the bathtub.

The underside of his shirt revealed Velcro inserts. "I fooled ya, didn't I?"

The Amish, I was to learn, are full of surprises.

FOUR HUNDRED THOUSAND DOLLARS!

Amos certainly surprised me. The forty-five-year-old farmer had saved four hundred thousand dollars over the course of twenty years, while renting a farm and raising fourteen children. When I visited Amos and his wife, Fern, and their

※ ※ ※

beautiful family, I looked for signs of stinginess, of a wife and children suffering somehow under the regime of a tight-fisted, straw-hatted Scrooge.

No one seems deprived; in fact, just the opposite. Amos and Fern's adorable children have a calmness and peace that I find striking and appealing. The Millers are a happy, thriving family, and Amos is a kind, loving father, who smiled fondly at his little ones as they climbed on and off his lap during our interviews. Fern told me that she's been checking out the fliers, looking for a sale on trampolines; this summer the little Millers are going to be bouncing and flipping to their hearts' content.

I tried every journalistic trick in the book to get Amos to impart pearls of wisdom, but it finally came down to this: "As far as our 'money secrets,' these are values handed down for generations—we can't take credit," he said.

And he's partly right. Thrift, common sense, wise money management, delayed gratification, etc., are taught from the time wee Moses and Mary are knee-high to a grasshopper. Amos can't boast about being thrifty any more than a child born into an Amish home could brag about knowing how to speak Pennsylvania Dutch. Money lessons are learned from the start of life.

Though he won't accept credit, Amos is definitely doing something right, and has been doing it—with Fern's help— for the last two decades.

Basically, Amos doesn't really know what he's done that's

✖ ✖ ✖

so remarkable. (The Plain humility is one more way the Amish are radically countercultural.)

"I've been around them a long time," said Banker Bill, "and the main thing that sets them apart, money-wise, is their values. They are upside down."

Kind of like the topsy-turvy English translation of some *Dietsch* sentences, like: "Jakie, throw Grampop down the stairs his hat." Or, "Ida, outten the light and make the door shut." And one more: "Buzzy, did you come over the hill down?"

Just which culture has things wrong side up?

It makes you wonder, just as we get the visual of poor Grampop lying on his head at the bottom of the stairs, just which culture has things wrong side up?

When compared to our *Englisher* money bungles, the Amish way of wealth is a whole inverted lifestyle of thrift, self-control, carefulness, sharing, and community. It's a curious prosperity—a rootedness, simplicity, and a step back to "quaint" money values—that goes way beyond debt-free living.

My peek at the Amish and their upside-down ways convinced me: they turn us Fancy folk on our excessive, overleveraged heads.

So how do we get turned right side up again?

The Amish can't teach us *one* golden piece of money wisdom that will help us live happy, contented lives while slowly but surely amassing gobs of cash like Amos did. On the contrary, there are about a dozen financial habits—money secrets—that we can pick up from folks like Amos (and Bishop Eli, Ephraim, Sadie, Naomi, et al.), spokes in a wheel that has been turning smoothly for centuries.

Hanging out with Amish folk such as Amos, I finally learned to pay attention to their habits and practices more than their words.

There was the old shovel, perfectly usable, with a piece of steel welded onto the handle, lying in the front flower bed ("You and I would have bought a new shovel a long time ago," Banker Bill pointed out). "We try and repair what we can," Amos said with a shrug.

Fern buys flour and sugar and other staples in fifty-pound bags from the Amish bulk food store, eliminating the middleman and saving scads over the years.

And as cherished as Lizzie, Eli, Katie, Sadie, and the rest are to their parents, Amos and Fern do not spoil them with a lot of extras. "We don't buy them whatever they want," Amos said.

When the work is done and the cows are milked, the Millers have fun together, playing badminton and making soft pretzels and homemade ice cream. The gentle tempo of their simple lifestyle seemed like soothing music to me.

Amos, you may not be willing to give yourself a pat on the back, but I give you all the credit in the world. Now all we have to do is figure out how to apply your tips (or "non-tips," as it were) to our own lives, and we'll be on our way to standing financially upright once again.

※ ※ ※

2

UWMW: USE IT UP, WEAR IT OUT, MAKE DO, OR DO WITHOUT

It took creativity, duct tape, and some stuffing of shame, but our bashed-in, totaled minivan looks pretty good.

It's my best example of "making do," one of the Amish community's most fantastic ways of saving money.

"Use it up, wear it out, make do, or do without," said Andy, the Amish boat cover maker, with a big smile. He's not the first guy to spout that maxim, but the Plain folk really take it to heart, and so they save big.

⚒ ⚒ ⚒

The Amish are keen menders, going to great lengths to fix what is broken, patch what is torn, and repair what is repairable.

I like the dictionary definition of *mend*: "to restore something to satisfactory condition," or "to improve something or make it more acceptable." But that's not the American way.

We ladies and gentlemen of the World often think nothing of chucking our less-than-fabulous cars/clothes/furniture/you name it and replacing them with new cars/clothes/furniture at the first sign of wear and tear. We like our things to be new and shiny, because most people are essentially like birds. (Yes, birds, flapping our wings excitedly whenever we spy something glossy and gleaming.) And after watching the Amish, and seeing their patched pants, darned socks, refurbished equipment, and even mended fences, I realized I was being a bit of a birdbrain myself by not "making do" much more often.

> We like our things to be new and shiny.

I can't sew on a button (though I learned to thread a needle in Pioneer Girls years ago), and I'm about as handy as the cast of *The Real Housewives of New York City*. But I did find out that I was pretty darn dexterous with a roll of tape.

Besides, making do is more of a mental exercise anyway. Can I emotionally deal with a wood-paneled microwave, a camera that's been dropped one too many times, or the world's ugliest tray tables? That was the real question.

✖ ✖ ✖

So I took stock, listing things in my home that had more "wear" left in them, and committed to making them last. But it wasn't long before my main revamp project became abundantly clear. One morning, on my way to the bank, I was rear-ended by a genius in a conversion van, yapping away on his cell phone. Well, he rear-ended a guy in an SUV—with tow hooks poking out the front—and *that* guy rear-ended me. *Boom! Crunch! Ugh.*

Other than a little whiplash and a seriously shaken psyche (I have a little PTSD from previous, serious car accidents), I was okay. But the van, a 2000 Oldsmobile Silhouette, was definitely on the bubble. It was never going to win a beauty contest anyway, but now the vehicle was uglier than sin, pockmarked with two twin holes in the back bumper, where the SUV driver's tow hooks had punctured them.

Surprisingly, it was still drivable, and I drove off to the banker anyway.

Soon we learned that our trusty white van was totaled. I immediately thought this meant that we were going to have to take out a loan for a "new" used van, since our savings were scraping, as Bishop Eli said, the bottom of the barrel because we were moving. Truth be told, I was tempted to get another van, even if it meant a car loan we couldn't afford. Though I had never been "car proud," as they say (once I had to be told what "detailing" was because I had no idea), it's one thing to drive an older-model car with tinges of rust, and another to drive the Unsightlymobile.

❊ ❊ ❊

And if I can be very shallow for a moment here, it didn't help matters that our son plays hockey in the city's wealthiest area (not because we live there, but because it's close-ish and has a great hockey program). It was hard for me not to feel self-conscious about driving into that parking lot six times a week and parking that dreadful-looking, aged, smashed-in clunker beside thirty-five-thousand-dollar SUVs.

This is where I needed to just suck it up and try to rise above it.

The Amish, with their upside-down values, would probably look at my van and think highly of me, although this was small comfort to me when I parked by a friend's sparkling new Volvo. "We admire someone with a new car or a new house," said Banker Bill. "But the Amish look at this completely differently. They look favorably on someone who is not living ostentatiously, but is instead living a modest and simple life. If someone is living high off the hog, the Amish would look at him and think he was abandoning their faith."

Unsightly though it may be, we drove that car another seven months before we finally figured out a cheap way to give it a little makeover. Doyle, my husband, helped a friend of ours—a body-shop guy—replace the crumpled van door with a new door. The brilliant "Grandpa George" also artfully covered the four-inch holes with white duct tape to match the van. Our cost? For parts, $120, a whopping

⌗ ⌗ ⌗

savings of $3,880, as we would have spent around $4,000 on a comparable used van. Oh, the tape is visible to the naked eye, but just barely. I love it!

Like I said, that was the major "make do" project in our lives, but there were definitely more where that came from.

FANCY DOIN'S

Andy's business making and repairing boat covers and re-upholstering boat seats turned out to be one of those enterprises that prospers during a national money pinch. "You can't sell a boat for its value these days," he said. "People are hanging on to their boats because they can't sell them. Instead, they are fixing their boats up, repairing their canvases and having the seats reupholstered."

In short, people are making do with their old boats, so Andy's business dovetails perfectly with his Amish ideals.

In a recession, though, even us Fancy folk are finding ways to "make it work," as *Project Runway*'s fashion design mentor, Tim Gunn, likes to tell his designer contestants. Here are a few ways regular people are doing just that:

- Caryn: "Instead of paying $90 for a compost bin at Home Depot, I used a plastic bin (we had paid $4 for it) and poked holes in it. I do have to go out and stir it myself. Who knows if it'll work well in the long term, but I feel pretty thrifty."

⌗ ⌗ ⌗

- Erin: "Just yesterday I needed (desperately) to mow the lawn, and the lawn mower is not functioning all of a sudden. I tried to fix it, but I don't know enough about small engine repair. I know we'll fix it later this week when we have time to take it all apart, but in the meantime the grass was shamefully long. I pulled out the manual push mower (you know, the kind that doesn't require gas) and cut the grass today. It doesn't look great, but it is (mostly) shorter."

- Lorna: "Early in our marriage, when we didn't have an extra penny to our names, I would darn my socks. I didn't have a wooden mold that you are supposed to put in your socks while you're darning (like my grandma did) so I put a lightbulb into my sock to help me do some pretty fine handiwork!"

- Linda: "I had a pair of jeans that started to fray at the bottom hem, so I trimmed them up about five inches, and now they are pretty cool cut-off capris. I'm thinking of finding some flashy ribbon at the fabric store to stitch across the edge to keep them from getting more cut-off shag. Also, I save, then reuse, the plant containers from new plants so when it's time to divide others, I have something to put them in, then give them away."

- Denise: "For years I didn't have an electric mixer because I had found a little handheld one (the kind that you crank by hand really fast) at a garage sale, and

⚒ ⚒ ⚒

it worked just fine. The bonus was that I got a workout every time I used it!"

- Tracey: "I use the paper from my kids' art easel after it has been painted or drawn on for wrapping paper."
- Hezra: "We have five kids, so we pass clothes between several families. Our kids are all different ages, enough that it usually works. But we have specific kids our hand-me-downs go to; then they circle back. We seriously have some of the girls' clothes that have been through seven girls." (Hezra's tip is super Amish. Every Amish mom I talked to said she either passed on clothes her children had grown out of, or used clothes that have been passed on from family and friends.)
- Ellie: "When we lived overseas, we would come home every summer and bring a whole lot of stuff back with us. One summer we had two backpacks and two pieces of luggage. Our suitcases were so full of books and other heavy items that we had to pay over $700 because we were a few pounds over our limit. We panicked, and then went into problem-solving mode. We asked for a huge plastic bag, then put the two backpacks in the bag, making it one piece of luggage. Then I ran up to the second floor and bought the cheapest little knapsack I could find. It turned out to be $17. We stuffed all our heaviest items into that little bag. We again had four pieces of luggage, all under the

※ ※ ※

weight limit. We saved ourselves $683 by improvising and reorganizing our packing. With a little creativity there's always a way around a problem!"

Caryn made the most of a plastic bin and kept $86 in her wallet, $86 that could be in Home Depot's cash register, while Ellie got real creative real fast, and the result was a savings of $683. Incredible! As Daniel Miller, a sharp young Amishman, likes to say, "My dad always said, 'It's either my money or it's theirs. I prefer it to be mine.'"

> So often, when we start thinking in terms of "Use it up, wear it out, make do, or do without," we *keep* more and more greenery in our bank accounts.

So often, when we start thinking in terms of "Use it up, wear it out, make do, or do without," we *keep* more and more greenery in our bank accounts, and *keep out* that same lucre from the bankrolls of home improvement stores and car dealerships.

Seeing the hard numbers from Caryn's and Ellie's make-do success stories caused me to ponder how many dollars I could be saving by really, truly "using it up."

A quick survey of my household items yielded a few things I could put to use (or put up with, more like it) awhile longer:

⌗ ⌗ ⌗

- A digital camera. We bought it new a few years ago, and since then it's been dropped a few times by overzealous kids and *doppich* (clumsy) Mom. It's way clunkier than the sleek, pretty, new models, but more than that, the battery compartment has to be closed by duct tape or it will slide open and the batteries will fall out. Also, for some reason the dial turns on with the slightest motion, so slight we don't even notice it, and as a result, we are always out of battery juice, an incredibly annoying thing when a beautiful Kodak moment unfolds. Still, a comparable camera, bought new, would be $170.
- The world's ugliest tray tables. We got these tray tables for a wedding present, in 1991, and they were ugly even then. Oh, these aren't plain wooden tables with a few scuffs. No sirree. These are microcosms of every bad fad that ever afflicted the late eighties and early nineties. The only thing missing on these tables is a photo of a guy with a mullet. They do, however, have a bold, unforgettable motif of stylized swans and bulrushes, with a palette of dove grey, dusty rose, powder blue, and a shock of black lacquer to just give the whole effect some focus. What I'm telling you is, they are ugly to the point of being fascinatingly so. Perhaps the Smithsonian will want them if they ever do an exhibit called

✖ ✖ ✖

Ghastly Home Décor from the Early Nineties. In the meantime, we can always throw a tea towel over them and call it good. Cost to buy a new set of tray tables: $40–$179.

- A wood-paneled microwave. Why don't we have a normal microwave? It's a long story. The one we do have is also, like the tray tables, a throwback to days of yore. It's like a small station wagon that warms things up, from the late seventies, when "high-speed cooking" was nifty. Anyway, about three years ago, our then two-year-old pushed her musical table over to the microwave, hopped up on it, pulled the knob off, and nuked it. When I got out of the shower, the house smelled like charred plastic. Since she was prone to such "mad scientist" operations, we decided to keep the microwave and simply turn the metal stick center of the knob with pliers. ("Pliers?" said a friend of mine, when I told her the story. "I see you, and I raise you.") We still use pliers to this day, because up until recently, our scientist did not have the manual dexterity to operate the pliers. Once, she tried to cook some noodles and went about five minutes over the allotted time because she couldn't turn off the microwave. The whole house smelled like charred food. Now every time we microwave anything, the unit gives off the stench of a nasty convenience store. Doyle: "It smells like someone has been smoking cigarettes inside that thing for twenty years." Cost of a new microwave: $65–$202.

As Freeman the goat guy said, "We try and make do, but then sometimes my boys will say, 'Datt [Dad], it's too long since this has been new,' and they are usually right." Obviously, it's been too long since our microwave was new, and I think we will be browsing the fliers for a replacement.

To this list of not-quite-worn-out items, I would add luggage (darn those cats and their claws!)—new: $100–$300; a cell phone (mine's positively antediluvian)—new: $99.99; and an alarm clock radio I think Doyle brought into our marriage—new: $19.99. If I hold out until these items actually do die a natural death, I would be "making do" big time, keeping a minimum $495 of my money. (Well, $495 minus $65, because the microwave is verging on the unendurable, and after thirty years of reheating service, we want to put the old gal out to pasture while she still has a shred of dignity.)

Four hundred-*plus* bucks! I like the sound of that! Just hearing the number gave me major oomph in my quest to "use it up" like the Amish do.

How about you? How much money could you keep by using things up until they are truly worn-out? I guarantee when you tally up your own list and dollar amount, you'll be happy you did.

⚹ ⚹ ⚹

AMISH HOME REMEDIES

The baby's colicky, it's 10:30 at night, and it's raining—what to do? The Amish certainly wouldn't hitch up their buggies and make a Walgreens run; they would "make do," naturally, with items mostly attainable in their cupboards, gardens, and cellars (in baby's case, they prescribe one teaspoon of fennel tea every thirty minutes to an hour). *Home Remedies from Amish Country* boasts more than six hundred tonics and tinctures, salves and supplements, to cure everything from fussy babies to gallstones. Some of the highlights:

- For "anemia": "Put 1 T. blackstrap molasses in a cup of hot water and drink. Take this mixture every day until you feel more energetic," asserts Mrs. Andy J. Byler.
- For "fluid retention": Lizzie Yoder swears by drinking one cup of horsetail tea a day.
- For cataracts: "Use better than half of honey and Heinz Vinegar (slightly more than one part honey to one part vinegar), put a few drops in eyes, it hurts but saves money," claims Amos Miller.

※ ※ ※

- Laxative: "Take one pinch of Epsom salt for three days," says Gideon Gingerich. "I had very good results with this."
- Insect stings: "To ease the pain, mix a teaspoon of unseasoned meat tenderizer with a few drops of water to make a paste and then place this on the injury," says John Eicher. "This will give your child almost instantaneous relief since an enzyme in meat tenderizer dissolves the toxins the insect has injected with its stinger."

—*Home Remedies from Amish Country* (Millersburg, OH: Abana Books, 2005)

Four Ways to Make Do

1. Shop Your Own Closet

The Amish don't have to deal with the matter of things going in and out of fashion, because, of course, a cape and kapp never go out of fashion in Leola, Pennsylvania! But the concept of looking at what you already have, clothing-wise, and shuffling things around a bit to get more mileage out of them? That's garbing yourself on the cheap, something the ladies of Leola would endorse.

❊ ❊ ❊

Now, before you huff and puff and say you know what's already in your closet, and that would be nothing to wear, give this tip a whirl, girl. According to "Serena" of the penny-pinching blog Style on a String (www.stylestring.com), there's a method to the madness of shopping in your own closet. Her words of wisdom:

"The first step is to organize your closet so you can find everything easily. Treat it like your own personal store. Arrange it by clothing type (T-shirts, dresses, jackets), then by color (think Taylor on *The Rachel Zoe Project!*). After you're organized, you can start seeing different ideas of what you could mix and match."

By trying this tip, I found that my newish mint green cardigan goes stunningly with a four-year-old brown satin camisole top. Who knew? I do, now! When I wore it to church with dress pants last Sunday, I felt like I had a spiffy new outfit on.

"You've only got one pair of feet anyway," Serena continues. "So make what you've got, the best that you've got . . . Only buy items that are classic, basic staples before you start experimenting. If you're looking for a pair of knee-high brown boots, start with a flat, simple, plain-looking pair that will go with everything. You can always enhance your shoe wardrobe later, but if you're missing the basics, you won't be able to tie together your pieces."

Preach it, sister!

And finally, "don't buy anything unless it is really different

※ ※ ※

than what you've got. So don't buy another sweater that you already have 5 duplicates of."

Who would buy five of the same look? I must admit, before the Amish thrift started to sink in, I routinely would like a certain trend and end up with far too many of the same sort of thing (hello, ruffles!). Check out page 148 for a creative way to weed out some overindulgences and possibly get free new-to-you clothes. Because, as Serena said, "Style has nothing to do with money"; shopping your own closet is green, frugal, and fabulous!

2. Shop Your Own Home

You might be surprised at how many cool finds are already there. According to Nate Berkus, home design expert, the greatest hurdle to jump for "home" shoppers is that once we find a space for something, we never even think of moving it.

"Walk into your bedroom and think, 'Would that dresser look great in my dining room? Can I take these lamps off my table and use them next to my sofa?'" Berkus advises, because, as he points out, "nothing is nailed down" ("DIY Home Makeovers: Light on Cash, Heavy on Creativity," *The Oprah Winfrey Show*, August 13, 2009, www.oprah.com/home/ Nate-Berkus-Tips-for-Budget-Home-Makeovers).

Almost immediately, I envisioned the perfect spot for a neglected lamp and gave it a new home where it positively glowed. After years of collecting dust on a bedroom chest of drawers, my marvelous 1930s-inspired lamp got

※ ※ ※

a new lightbulb and lit up a gloomy space atop an antique steamer trunk lugged across the ocean and the prairies by my Mennonite forebears. Beautiful! I felt exactly as though I had gotten a new lamp.

Shanna, from the *wonderful* blog My Favorite Everything (www.myfavoriteeverything.com), had a similar experience, moving an armoire she had bought in college from her bedroom to her daughter's room, which had no closet. Her husband added a closet rod inside the armoire. Freeing up space in her own bedroom, Shanna swapped out a smaller armoire, and it became a TV stand.

"I wanted to show you that in de-cluttering and reorganizing, you don't necessarily have to go out and buy something new," she told her readers in a 2009 post. "Sometimes you can shop in your own house and find a solution (Did you hear that, Honey? I didn't buy anything to complete these projects—well we did buy the felt moving pads, $11. And the closet rod, $4.)" (www.myfavoriteeverything.com/2009/baby/put-your-helmut-on-and-get-ready-for-2010).

Talk about making do. So *schmart*!

3. Grocery Shop Your Own Cupboards

Instead of going out to buy new groceries or ordering takeout, build dinner around what's in the fridge, pantry, or freezer already. I know, I know, a rotisserie chicken sounds sublime right now, but unless you only have a jar of mayo, a Diet Coke, and half a box of bran cereal, you can most likely

❈ ❈ ❈

get creative and save some cash. I mean, if I can do it, you certainly can!

Let's say you did grab a rotisserie chicken a couple of days ago. It's not going to feed a whole family for a second night. How about some chicken quesadillas or soup? There's broccoli, eggs, and some shredded cheese. What to make? You've got most of the ingredients for a crustless quiche.

Don't feel like cooking? Me neither, sometimes! So I have started to keep family-size cans of tomato and chicken noodle soup on hand, plus bread and cheese, so we can whip together a no-effort meal of soup and grilled cheese sandwiches. About half the time, having easy stuff on hand curbs the urge to make a pricey run to the deli or call the pizza man.

I challenged myself with this idea a few days ago. Groceries were low, but I didn't want to spend twenty dollars on pizza. I made myself look at every row of the pantry, even the bottom row, with its cans of beans and things, the stuff I usually buy for a recipe and then end up not using for some reason. I knew I had brown sugar, molasses (enough for a gingerbread man convention), and two big cans of beans—your basic baked beans ingredients. When I saw the box of Jiffy mix jammed into the corner of the pantry, I knew the Craker family's dinner destiny: brown sugar–baked beans and cornbread. It was simple, tasty, filling—and economical (about eighty cents per person!).

The meal reminded me of Ella Yoder and her favorite frugal meal in the dead of winter: "Tomato soup, made with

※ ※ ※

canned tomato juice, milk, and a little butter—it's my husband's favorite." She utilized what she had on hand, and the result was make-do noshing at its finest.

The average American household spends 42 percent of its total food budget on dining out. Grocery shopping in your own home helps you eat out less, especially when you brown-bag your lunch instead of eating out.

4. Fix It and Forget It

No, I'm not talking about Crock-Pot cooking, though that is a little addiction of mine. (You mean you can dump five things in a pot, turn on a button, and—voilà!—dinner is served? That's not even cooking—it's can opening!)

In our first year as landlords of our previous house, we have learned that fixing stuff, either ourselves or by employing a pro, is super economical. Now, did I mention that I am just not handy in any sense of the word? Doyle's fairly handy, but he doesn't know how to get a dryer to start behaving like a dryer, not a lint trap that rolls our clothes around for an hour and leaves them damp.

This year, we've called the appliance guy three or four times, between our two houses. First, the dryer got worse, and I thought it was on death's door. Clothes had to be run through the cycle four or five times before they were reasonably dry. But much to my delight, the appliance guy worked on it for fifteen minutes and declared it good for the next ten years. Cost: $100. New dryer: starting at $300. Savings: $200.

⚒ ⚒ ⚒

Similar scenarios unfolded for the fridge (something about a coil) and the oven (it smelled like gas—very bad!).

Fridge repair: $120. New fridge: starting at $400. Savings: $280.

Oven repair: $40 (it was "just a wire"). New oven: starting at $400. Savings: $360.

Total cost of repairs: $260. Total cost to replace the appliances new: $1,100. Total savings: $840.

(Of course, if you and yours happen to know how to replace fridge coils, etc., you could keep the entire $1,100.)

Doyle recently fixed our portable DVD player ($119.99 new), and now that I'm keeping track, I'm sure his fix-its over the years have saved us tons of money. But even if you don't have a DIY (do-it-yourself) bone in your body, as you can see, sometimes calling the appliance repair people can be a low-cost way to "make do." Talk about "restoring something to satisfactory condition," and "improving something or make it more acceptable"! What's more acceptable than a large wad of cash, un-parted from the warmth and safety of your wallet?

Sadie Says . . .

"We use things until they wear out," said Sadie. "It's that simple."

Over and over again, the Plain people told me how they save money by truly wearing things out and getting the most possible use out of them. These are the folks who cobbled a working maple syrup evaporator ($3,000, new) out of scrap heap finds. They are without a doubt the most resourceful, adaptive, and imaginative culture out there. It's all about being thoughtful and careful about spending.

And it is rather simple, once you start thinking like the Amish, and making "UWMD" (Use It Up, Wear It Out, Make Do, or Do Without) a mantra in your life. Once you start tallying up the amount of money you're *keeping*, you'll be all over it like lint in a broken dryer.

✕ ✕ ✕

MY AMISH MONEY MAKEOVER

The Amish use things until they wear out—completely. This means they keep a surprisingly big amount of money that we *Englishers* routinely hand over to the store.

To Do:

1. Make a list of five items you would like to replace with new, but won't just yet because you are becoming a paragon of thrift! Calculate the cost of replacing those items, and sport a big, sassy grin on your frugal face.
2. This week, try shopping in your own closet, home, and pantry, and save $$$$.

_____

_____

_____

_____

_____

※ ※ ※

3

DON'T EAT THE MARSHMALLOW: LEARNING DELAYED GRATIFICATION

Ah, the famous marshmallow study of the 1960s.

You know the one. A group of four-year-olds were put in a room with just a chair and a table. Given the option of picking either a marshmallow, a cookie, or a pretzel stick, most chose the gooey, fluffy marshmallow.

Then came the hard part. The children were told they could eat one marshmallow immediately, or, if they waited until the researcher left and returned again, they could have two gooey, fluffy marshmallows.

Some little ones popped the prize into their mouths before the researcher even shut the door behind him. *Two marshmallows? Who cares? I have one delicious treat right in front of me, and I am going to eat it right now because it looks super yummy.* Their pint-sized brains were whirring.

Unfortunately, the same kind of thinking has tripped me up many, many times.

"Shoes! Fabulous shoes! Right in front of me? I must have them!"

Indulgence *now*—it's the bane of our culture's financial existence.

We want what we want when we want it, kind of like those drooling four-year-olds in the study. "It is human nature to want it and want it now; it is also a sign of immaturity," wrote Dave Ramsey in his book *Total Money Makeover* (3rd ed.). "Being willing to delay pleasure for a greater result is a sign of maturity" (Nashville: Thomas Nelson, 2009, 17).

The children in the marshmallow study were tracked for years by the researchers, who found that those munchkins who wrestled with temptation but found a way to resist grew up to be better adjusted, had less behavioral problems, and scored an average of 210 points higher on the SAT test.

Delayed gratification is a particularly fine quality of the Amish, who are major long-term thinkers. Take Ella.

"We rented a farm our first twenty years of marriage," she

✖ ✖ ✖

told me as I sat in her kitchen and watched her bake, the sweet aromas of juicy apples, sugar, and butter drifting deliciously from her stove. "Renting seems like a dead horse, but we had to do it that way.

"There were a lot of things we wanted to do but didn't do," she went on. "Some women would not be happy with that—just spending on what was absolutely necessary. I would have loved to have linoleum floors and a sun porch for my sewing machine. It never happened. I just waited.

"We focused," she concluded, "on buying a farm."

Talk about big-picture thinking! Ella (and her Amish friends) probably would have been in the group that resisted the one marshmallow and were rewarded with two.

I can't help but think the Amish would have also made their own squishy orbs of sugar and gelatin, possibly grinding the collagen themselves from the hooves of their farm animals. Let's not put it past them.

I tried making homemade marshmallows one Christmas, and my children are still horrified by the memory. Imagine, if you will, a slimy slab of tofu infused with the sweetness of a thousand packets of Splenda. That's how well that worked out.

But I digress.

It's a core idea in Amish culture that you wait for what you want, which in many cases is a farm for your children and grandchildren. "We are taught not to just buy whatever we please, but rather to work and save to pay for it," Bishop Ephraim told me.

※ ※ ※

It seems so simple. But apparently, our culture seems to have the patience of a drooling four-year-old. Okay, so *I* have the patience of a drooling four-year-old. Are you happy now? But so do you, probably. I'm just saying . . .

Delaying gratification is tricky, experts believe, for the same reason that diets often hit the skids. The brain has a hard time accepting the trade-off of instant delight (eating or spending) for abstract, far-off goals, such as looking reasonably presentable in a swimsuit or having money in the bank for a rainy day.

Back to marshmallows: would you be able to wait a year to get a thousand dollars versus getting five hundred bucks today? Ooh, that's a tough one. But if we do exercise that kind of self-control, then we probably won't buy things on credit cards because we see something and want it. Learning delayed gratification means being able to save money toward a vacation next year, a college education in ten years, and a retirement that may be decades away.

One of my biggest issues with postponing the purchase of what I crave today and, instead, saving for what I want in ten years is that my goals are rather vague and flabby. A few years ago, I told my dad that I was going to go to Vancouver for the 2010 Olympics. It kind of annoyed me when he said, "Start putting away money now" rather than "That would be really fun!" Apparently, I had this fuzzy notion that the money would pour in at the right time.

But guess what? It turns out, you really do reap what you

※ ※ ※

sow. In four years' time, I frittered away any extra cash that may have been socked away for an Olympic trip on shoes, dresses, books, lamps, pedis, pizza—you get the picture. When it came time to plunk down a few thousand dollars for a Vancouver trip, there was no money in that fund. In fact, there was no fund! There was no great, shining Olympic moment for me either (and it's too late to take up speed skating now).

However, when we are focused on a goal, like buying a farm someday or, like Sara, taking a great anniversary trip, that clarity of purpose can help us say no to all kinds of things:

> In four years' time, I frittered away any extra cash that may have been socked away for an Olympic trip on shoes, dresses, books, lamps, pedis, pizza— you get the picture.

> Sara: "When Drew and I first got married, we were dirt-poor! We survived on mac 'n' cheese and frozen pizza, and it was only through a dear friend who paid me a borderline-exorbitant amount to hang out with her child after work that we had gas money. Somehow, though, we managed to save three thousand dollars in one year for a first anniversary trip to Maine. We used part of the money

✖ ✖ ✖

to buy a set of bikes and a rack for our car so we could take the bikes with us.

During that first year (and I think a couple after that), we had no cell phones, no Internet, no date nights; but man, did we have one awesome first anniversary trip. It was definitely worth the scrimping!"

What is "worth the scrimping" to you? When you know what that is—a special vacation, a kitchen remodel, a hybrid car, a summer cottage—you can take aim at having it someday by saying no to yourself regularly in the everyday.

This is definitely another "thrift muscle" that needs to have a regular workout. A highly disciplined friend from college once told me he made it a practice to say no to himself once a day. Whether it was forgoing fast food, not watching too much TV, or refusing to spend money on something frivolous, he felt the practice helped him be more disciplined in all areas of his life.

> You can take aim at having it someday by saying no to yourself regularly in the everyday.

I don't know about you, but I feel a little burst of energy and self-respect when I say no to flippant spending. Yet when I cave in and buy something on a whim, or something I don't

※ ※ ※

really need, I feel a little sick, as if I overindulged at the amusement park, inhaling a deep-fried Twinkie when a fudge bar would have sufficed.

When I exercise a little self-control, I end up being glad I did. A couple of summers ago, I was in a high-end department store and saw a sundress I absolutely adored on sight. It was, as they say, screaming my name. However, when I dashed over to see how much that gorgeous thing would set me back, I was halted in my tracks. Seventy-nine dollars, for a sundress! Well, there was no way I could justify that. "I'll wait for it to go on sale," I told myself bravely—*Buck up, little camper*—and marched out of the store, a little deflated, yet also feeling that pop of verve that only a display of willpower can deliver.

A couple of weeks later, I was in a lower-end store (much lower-end) and noticed a very pretty sundress in all my favorite colors. It was fourteen dollars—totally justifiable! Can I tell you that low-end sundress became one of my favorite things to wear for two summers? And the compliments! My word, it got embarrassing. Well, maybe it wasn't that drastic, but I did get lots of praise for that fourteen-dollar sundress.

The pricey frock? I went back a few times, but I never did catch it on sale. Besides, by the next summer, the trend was over—way over. I had wrestled, resisted, and triumphed in the end. I should definitely try that more often.

Experts say it all starts when you're young. In chapter 2, I talk about how the Amish teach delayed gratification as a

※ ※ ※

matter of course to their children from the time they are small. So when Moses and Mary grow up and hitch their buggies together, they won't be making many thoughtless and trivial purchases.

Walter Mischel, the Stanford professor of psychology in charge of the marshmallow experiment, was quoted in a 2009 *New Yorker* article: "'This is where your parents are important,'" he said. "'Have they established rituals that force you to delay on a daily basis? Do they encourage you to wait? And do they make waiting worthwhile?' According to Mischel, even the most mundane routines of childhood—such as not snacking before dinner, or saving up your allowance, or holding out until Christmas morning—are really sly exercises in cognitive training: we're teaching ourselves how to think so that we can outsmart our desires" (Jonah Lehrer, "Don't!" *New Yorker*, May 19, 2009, 6).

Parents, we can teach our kids that waiting can be wonderfully worthwhile and give them a gift for life. But even if our own parents never taught us how to "outsmart our desires," there's no time like today to apply a little "delay training."

How can we say no to the marshmallows that keep popping up front and center on our radars?

THINK ABOUT SOMETHING ELSE

I imagine Ella, Sadie, Amos—all of them focused for years on buying farms—trained themselves to think about the pot of

❊ ❊ ❊

gold at the end of that long and tedious rainbow: the family farm.

Dr. Mischel, after umpteen hours of observation, realized the patient kids had a crucial skill that the hasty tots did not. He called it "strategic allocation of attention." Instead of getting infatuated with the marshmallow—the "hot stimulus," he called it—the enduring children sidetracked their attention from the yummy treat and pretended to play hide-and-seek under the desk or sang songs from their favorite TV show.

"If you're thinking about the marshmallow and how delicious it is, then you're going to eat it," Mischel said. "The key is to avoid thinking about it in the first place" (Lehrer, 3).

So don't think about those shoes! Instead, visualize yourself lying in a hammock in Fiji, or entertaining dignitaries in your fabulous remodeled kitchen.

Fritter Not, My Friend

Even the word *fritter* is a fun, sugary word—delicious, even, coated in batter and deep-fried. But there's nothing delicious about blowing money mindlessly. It can deep-fry you, though. Check out your bank statement and see how much money you simply fritter away on impulsive little things, like ice cream and pizza and magazines and lattes and (fill in the blank).

My weakness is lattes. Talk about a "hot stimulus." A

✖ ✖ ✖

tall mocha latte from a coffeehouse is $3, and I could pretty much have one every day. Now let's do the math:

$3 x 5 = $15 per week.

$15 x 4 = $60—*$60 a month for coffee!*

It gets worse.

$60 x 12 = $720.

What could I buy with $720? Where do I start? A new microwave, among other things, maybe?

> Check out your bank statement and see how much money you simply fritter away on impulsive little things.

Even if I treated myself to one latte per week and skipped the other four, I would still be in the black $576. Furthermore, I could make my own lattes at home for super cheap (one pound of coffee yields about forty-five 8-ounce cups; even a premium brand, such as Starbucks, at $11.99 a pound, would generate forty-five cups of joe at $0.26 a pour).

It's shocking, I tell you, to discover the lavish dissipation of one's frittering. When you think about it, this is merely like saying no a few times a day to *mini* marshmallows. It will be wonderful practice for when you are faced with a regulation-size, air-puffed temptation. So fire up that old dust-gathering cappuccino machine you got for a wedding present, and fritter not, my friend.

Still Want it?

Here's a canny formula for calculating the true value of something you really, really want. Say you fall in love with a $100 pair of shoes. Try this simple math before you do anything rash: Write down your pretax income (say, $40,000), subtract 25 percent for taxes ($10,000), and divide what's left ($30,000) by 2,000 (the hours you work in a year). At $15 an hour, you'd need to work seven hours for those shoes. Are they still worth it?

Small Luxuries

You'll notice I said I would still be buying myself one latte per week. Hey, a girl has to treat herself once in a while, right? I'm a firm believer in the idea that a small indulgence here and there can get someone over the hump. Just as a chocolate kiss can tide me over when I'm suffering from a cocoa bean craving, sometimes a teensy trinket serves to restore my willpower so I won't spend more than I can afford.

No need to quit spending cold turkey—just *cool* turkey.

The Amish, a people of stone-cold impulse control, don't really understand the concept of wee indulgences. Bishop Jake, for example, didn't get it when I asked him what his idea of a "small luxury" was.

"Let's say you wanted to treat yourself with a little something special," I said, smiling and nodding encouragingly.

His Chihuahua (an Amish Chihuahua!), Rufus, began barking crazily.

"Ice cream," he said, sure that that would be it, and I would leave him and Rufus in peace. But every Amish person I asked this question had answered with ice cream.

"Besides ice cream?"

"Okay, now you're pushing me down low!" he said in exasperation, shaking his head in bewilderment. "Salad dressing! Now, that would be a treat!"

When I pressed Ella in a similar fashion, she eventually cracked. "Ritz." Yes, the crackers. She sighed happily at the thought. "I just *love* the Ritz. But we usually buy crackers in bulk. Or make our own."

Now when I see a box of Ritz crackers, I have to smile.

Seriously, the lady is pining for a four-dollar box of crackers! It just goes to show, money doesn't buy happiness, and the Amish know how to control impulses big and small.

Bishop Jake and Ella sure aren't going to squander their hard-earned money very often on a bottle of ranch dressing or a tin of buttery crackers, not when there's a farm to be saved for. But once in a while, they will let themselves have a little delicacy.

These modest "extravagances" made me think about recalibrating my own treat scale. Instead of a thirty-dollar T-shirt from a concert (and as an entertainment writer, I go to lots of concerts), maybe a ten-dollar mug will scratch the itch.

✖ ✖ ✖

Oh, but isn't that fritter city, lady? A ten-dollar mug? It *would* be frittering, if I also bought a three-dollar latte every day, a four-dollar glossy magazine per week, and another ten-dollar mug the next week when I went to a different show. If you can keep a lid on the small stuff, by tracking spending and saying no often, a delightful little something may actually keep you on task for the long haul.

Besides, it's a good thing to adjust our thinking when it comes to why, how, and how often we treat ourselves, especially when things are tight.

"In hard times, people look for different levels of luxury," explained Norman Love, founder of Norman Love Confections. "When you open a box of premium chocolates, you feel rich. I can buy two pieces of chocolate for $5. The Queen of England can't buy any better chocolate than you can" (Jacqueline Mitchard, http://www.parade.com/food/2010/02/14-why-the-world-needs-chocolate.html).

Chocolate, Ritz crackers, salad dressing—whatever gets your buggy going, a small dose of it might help you refocus on the big picture.

Ultimately, it all boils down to delaying gratification now for a big payoff later on. If, as Dr. Mischel said, "intelligence is largely at the mercy of self-control," the Amish are the *schmartest* people around (Lehman, 2).

The bottom line: focus on what you want in the future, and learn to say no to all those distracting, alluring, big, and small marshmallows right now.

※ ※ ※

Did you know there are actually T-shirts that say, "Don't eat the marshmallow"?

I want one of those shirts. But I think that purchase is just going to have to wait.

❇ ❇ ❇

MY AMISH MONEY MAKEOVER

The Amish say no to themselves on a regular basis. If they wore T-shirts with words on them, they could proudly wear "Don't Eat the Marshmallow" emblazoned over their thrifty hearts. They focus instead on the big picture, and the result is loads of un-frittered money in the bank.

To Do: Check out your bank statement and see how much money you simply fritter away on impulsive little things. Think about what kinds of impulsive purchases trip you up on a regular basis. Vow to kick the marshmallows in their cushy hind ends.

_____

_____

_____

_____

_____

※ ※ ※

4

PAY ON TIME

Bishop Ephraim Lapp is one sharp cookie. The self-taught accountant and financial consultant "knows more about Amish money secrets than anyone else I know," said Banker Bill.

He and his wife are avid readers, and at night, in their almost empty nest, the two settle in comfy chairs and read books by C. S. Lewis and J. R. R. Tolkien by the light of oil lamps. "It gets awful quiet around here in the evening," his wife, Nell, told me.

I also spied some interesting reading material on Ephraim's side table: *Think Like a Billionaire, Become a Billionaire*. Mild-mannered Ephraim has that wonderful Amish contentedness

⌘ ⌘ ⌘

about him; I'm quite sure he's not trying to become filthy rich.

But he is attempting to learn a thing or two about savvy money management. And one thing he and any billionaire can probably agree on is this: you pay your bills on time.

"To pay someone on time is an extension of the commandment 'Do not steal,'" he said serenely. "If it's due on the tenth, and you pay it on the fifteenth, you are stealing that man's money for five days."

Ephraim is completely relaxed about this, and why shouldn't he be? The Amish have a pristine record when it comes to faithful bill paying.

Banker Bill can vouch for this. He's never lost money on an Amish loan, *ever*. He's been doing business with the Plain people for twenty years, and has had countless thousands of loans and no problems. Bill said that this year, one guy was a few days late on one month's mortgage payment. Everyone else paid on time, every time. "If the guy's seven days late, if I need to, I'll go pull his beard," Bill said jovially. "But it almost never happens."

Naturally, if we are a few days late on something, you and I don't just have a jocular fellow such as Banker Bill "pull our beards"—we get slapped with nasty late charges.

I'm not the most together person in the world, and when life gets crazy, I have forgotten to pay on the right day more than once. Also, because we own two properties, if our renter doesn't pay on time, or if things are tighter than usual, I have been known to juggle things a bit, knowing both mortgage payments will be paid well before the fearsome thirty days late. I mean, hey, this kind of juggling only costs me $72 a month in late fees.

What? That's $864 a year!

Calm down. It's not that bad. See, if anything, it's usually only the rental property that's paid late—during the "grace period," you understand. This means I am only out $432 a year . . . a big enough chunk of change to go to a fabulous bed-and-breakfast with Lake Michigan views for the weekend.

Or hire a painter to paint my bedroom a magnificent shade of aqua.

Or take the family to see U2 in concert, so that someday they can tell their grandchildren they saw the Elvis and Beatles of the twenty-first century.

But apparently, I would rather fill a huge bucket with $1 bills and throw it in the creek by our house, laughing maniacally as the dollars floated away.

With apologies to Bishop Ephraim, I don't really agree that I am stealing from the mortgage company when I pay within thirty days and simply pay them an extra $36.

The only one I am stealing from is myself.

The mortgage company? They are probably praying my payment arrives late. A late payment to a credit card company is even better for the credit card company than an on-time payment. "If there was a way for them to legally delay all payments until after the due date, and then sock you for late fees, you can be sure that they would," wrote G. E. Miller on the blog 20somethingfinance.com. "That is how they make their money—and in these 'lean times' they are going to hang on to every dollar that they can squeeze out of you" ("How to Fight Late Fees & Bank Overdrafts," September 11, 2008, http://20somethingfinance.com/how-to-wipe-out-credit-card-late-fees-bank-overdrafts/).

I'd almost rather send that money floating down Plaster Creek.

Credit card companies are definitely the worst. Even if you pay your bill in full each month, they have tricks up their sleeves to stick it to you with late fees you don't even deserve.

Recently, I paid a balance on a clothing company credit card, using their online bill payment center. With a few clicks, the bill was paid and I never gave it another thought. A couple of weeks later, when reading over my bank statement, I realized the amount had never been deducted. Slightly nervous, I decided to give it a few days, since the bank had recently been bought out by another bank and there were a few delays in things posting.

When I got my bill, I was horrified to see that not only had my payment not been applied, but I had been fined $39 in late charges. *What?* I immediately got on the phone and explained that I had paid the bill on time, but somehow it never was taken out of my bank account. *A likely story,* I'm sure she was thinking.

※ ※ ※

"Did you write down your confirmation number?" the customer service rep asked suspiciously.

"Well, no, I just thought everything was fine," I said sheepishly. (Show of hands—who actually keeps track of twelve confirmation numbers a month?)

"We don't have the option to waive late fees," she said, with all the sympathy of a prison matron.

"But—but—" I was sputtering now. "I have never paid late before!"

That's where I was wrong. I *had* paid late before, she was delighted to inform me, almost a year prior to this incident. I had paid off the balance of my card, and—silly me—didn't think to open the bill when it came. Apparently, I had been charged with an annual fee of some kind, and when I didn't pay it, I was also charged a $39 late fee to add insult to injury.

Blech! Almost $80 in one year to this unsavory bunch of chuckleheads. That's just one more reason to get rid of all credit cards forever (see chapter 9). As they say, when you lie down with the dogs, expect to get up with fleas.

> Paying on time is one more way the Amish keep their money, and part of the reason they do so well at it is that they are highly motivated.

I figured some of these late fees, like the occasional late

payment on our rental property, were no big deal, because hey, it wasn't like our credit would be affected. But when I did the math, I realized any late fees are really unacceptable and to be avoided at all costs.

Paying on time is one more way the Amish keep their money, and part of the reason they do so well at it is that they are highly motivated. In fact, according to Erik Wesner, it's unthinkable to pay your bills after the due date.

"The right thing to do is to honor your debts, in an Amish man's mind," he told me. "Not doing so would be very shameful and, you could even argue, an un-Christian approach. Amish are taught early it is the right thing to do. Beyond that, there is likely a social incentive operating as well—if you were someone who did not honor his debts, that would get around pretty quickly. There is a sense of shame operating in this, that we may have lost to a degree."

While I'm not a fan of shame, I am a fan of wising up to smarter money habits (not to mention weekends on Lake Michigan, aqua walls, and Bono). I also appreciate the peace that comes with "honoring your obligations," as a young Amish farmer put it. So I decided to crack down. And predictably, sitting a little tighter for just a few days made it possible for me to pay every bill on time, and the resolve paid off. Not only did I have a gorgeous $72 to spend on whatever I wanted, or save it for something grander—that felt marvelous—I felt more relaxed about my whole money picture.

※ ※ ※

Bishop Ephraim has known this forever: relaxation comes from paying your bills on or before their due dates. Playing games with due dates was stressing me out, and I was losing those games every single month.

Stress + \$432 in the mortgage company's coffers = I'm a chucklehead too.

Peace + \$432 in my bank account = Lake Michigan, here I come.

⁂ ⁂ ⁂

MY AMISH MONEY MAKEOVER

There's nothing "Plain" about paying bills on time—it's a beautiful thing! While we *Englishers* often play games with due dates, the Amish almost always pay on time, every time.

TO DO: Think of a bill you sometimes pay late. Does the amount make you ill? Good! Hopefully you'll be motivated to sit tight and pay up. Think of something fantastic you could be spending that money on instead.

※ ※ ※

5

RETHINKING GIFTS

It's Maddie's first birthday, and the Yoders are going to honor the day.

My visit came in the middle of winter, and their farmhouse smells like wood smoke. Three wooden chairs sit in the large, Spartan living room, plus a bench and a desk.

The little Yoder girls, Maddie, one, and Susannah, two and a half, flash dimples at me, mischievously. They look adorable in their little dresses and bonnets, and Amos, three, is endearing as well in a bowl haircut and pint-sized suspenders. "We are going to have ice cream after supper to celebrate Maddie's birthday," her mother, Martha, said, smiling.

Ice cream? *Just* ice cream? Maddie (a short form of Martha)

※ ※ ※

is too young to know any better, but her older siblings must get presents on their birthdays, right?

"For Christmas or birthdays, we get them something they need, usually. Like Sarah got a new dress for Christmas," said Martha. "Or maybe we might get them a small toy, or a puzzle, or a game."

"One gift per child, then?" I asked, already marveling as I pictured my own children and the haul they get for birthdays and Christmas.

"Yes, of course," Martha said, slightly puzzled, as if to say, *Why would Abel and I get our seven children more than one gift?*

Why indeed? And the one gift bestowed is sure to be simple and inexpensive, not a $300 video game system or a $100 doll. "It's my daughter's fifth birthday, and we are getting her a coloring book," Sadie told me about her family.

Sadie's Lydia, however, likely received the coloring book with a happy spirit.

The Amish way of giving gifts was one thing that stopped me in my tracks. I love giving gifts as much as I love getting them—why, gifts are my love language! I'm talking about the best-selling book by Gary Chapman, *The 5 Love Languages: The Secret to Love That Lasts* (Thorndike Press, 2005). The key idea behind the book is basically simple. After many years of counseling, Dr. Chapman noticed a pattern: everyone he had ever counseled had a "love language," a primary way of expressing and interpreting love. My way of interpreting love, like many of you, no doubt, is gifts, giving and receiving them.

☡ ☡ ☡

This, of course, is a pricier love language than "words of affirmation" or "quality time."

I wanted to incorporate as much as I could from the Amish and their money habits, but how could I give up gifts? Well, according to Dr. Chapman, I might not have to give up gifts, just put more thought into what I'm giving: "Don't mistake [the gift] love language for materialism; the receiver of gifts thrives on the love, thoughtfulness, and effort behind the gift," he wrote on his Web site, www.5lovelanguages.com.

Whew! It's such a relief to know I'm not just a material girl, and that a gift well given doesn't have to cost a wad of dough.

> I wanted to incorporate as much as I could from the Amish and their money habits, but how could I give up gifts?

The first thing I needed to do was rethink the whole concept of gifts—what they should look like, where (as in, which stores) they should come from, and how much I should spend on them. How many gifts to give is also something to reconsider, especially at Christmas, the year's massive blowout gift-giving occasion.

GIFT GLUTTED

I'll never forget the Christmas when I realized my children were turning into little loot-snatching robots. Jonah, then six,

⌗ ⌗ ⌗

barely glanced at freshly opened presents before swiveling around to look for more gifts under the tree. Three-year-old Ezra's eyes were glazed over with the "gimmes," and there were still two more gift-giving occasions before Yuletide was a wrap. Doyle and I had to act, or the beauty, peace, and meaning of the season would be lost under a heap of plastic playthings and the frenzied accumulation thereof.

It didn't help one bit that both boys have birthdays in December (our daughter, adopted the following year from Korea, would also have a December birthday). The days between their birthdays and Christmas were like one big lazy Susan, spinning with toys for them. This brought the issue of curbing materialism into sharp focus for us as parents.

I'm not the only mom fed up with gift-glutted holidays. Every parent has been appalled at one time or another with the Christmas pile-up of plastic, batteries, and toy parts, some of them tossed to the side almost immediately and perhaps never touched again. A friend of mine recalled how, one year, her in-laws woke her exhausted preschooler, lying asleep in a heap of wrapping paper, to open more loot. Her daughter burst into tears, completely overwhelmed.

There has to be a better way, and since the keep-it-simple approach of the Amish was already influencing every spending decision I made, what better time to apply Plain money principles than Christmas?

Scale Back

"If children get into the toys and the gifts so much, they lose the meaning of the season," said Bishop Jake, father and grandfather of a multitude.

The first step in reprogramming how we think about Christmas gifts was to scale back. Obviously, Bishop Jake is right: too many toys rob our children of the spiritual riches of the season. Let's be honest: they rob us of the spiritual riches of the season too. And as the Amish show us, we simply don't need a bunch of presents to make us happy.

"We pick names at Christmas among the adults," said Naomi, the mother of several grown children. "My daughters and daughters-in-law really like LED lights, and the guys ask for the DeWalt flashlights." (Since LED lighting is not plugged in to an electrical source, the Amish can light their lamps and their buggies with it and still stay off the power grid.)

It seems austere by Fancy standards, but that's the Amish for you, keeping it simple and penny-wise in all things, even Christmas gifts.

Like Naomi's family, most Amish families pick names out of a hat and buy one Christmas gift for one family member each year. The mega-practical Plain people usually go for useful, need-based gifts, and sometimes these gifts are handmade. The lady of the house might receive something she can use in the home, such as cooking or sewing tools, while her husband might snag equipment for use in the barn or apparatuses for

❈ ❈ ❈

their horses. Older Amish girls might receive household items for their hope chests, such as china, quilts, and other housewares. Older Amish boys are likely to be given tools. Younger children will receive handmade clothes, rag dolls, wooden toys, or books. "Usually, we get the children something they need," said Sadie.

> I don't know if I'm prepared to receive only a lightbulb for Christmas . . . but I think we could all stand to dial it down about ten notches.

I don't know if I'm prepared to receive only a lightbulb for Christmas (okay, there's no way I'm prepared for that), but I think we could all stand to dial it down about ten notches. That's why, as a family, we Crakers are down to three gifts. Not quite Amish, but fairly restrained compared to what it could be. Years ago, we implemented the "principle of the three wise men": we each get something we want, something we need (an excellent slot for snow-pants, hockey equipment, and bookshelves), and a surprise. This Christmas, in a spirit of razing that toy pile even more, we aimed for two of the three categories to be (a) experiential or charitable, and (b) "homegrown" in some way.

It Doesn't Have to Come in a Box

One of the best antidotes to toy overload is "experiential"

gift giving. That is, instead of wrapping up a thirty-dollar, battery-powered stuffed animal that makes noises, only to have the thing break within a week (true story), you give the gift of a single experience, shared or not, of know-how, skill, and most of all, a memory. We gave Jonah, our hockey nut, tickets to a Grand Rapids Griffins game ($60), and Ezra a year's membership to the Grand Rapids Art Museum ($50). Neither one was cheap, but the art museum membership was actually a fantastic value. He and a parent can get in the museum anytime for free, and participate weekly in the Saturday Family Arts program, featuring activities and crafts.

Grandma Doreen is known for giving experiences such as horseback riding lessons, music lessons, memberships to museums, and tickets to the ballet or the theater to her little angels. "Experiences are the enriching gift of a lifetime. When we think back on our childhoods, we carry forward that memory, that ability learned, forever. Compare that to a toy," she said.

Of course, this isn't necessarily a money-saving tip—experiential gifts can be very expensive—but giving this kind of gift enriches your family's bond, not just the toy box. It's an investment in relationships,

> It's an investment in relationships, rather than electronics and toys, an idea completely in line with Amish abundance.

rather than electronics and toys, an idea completely in line with Amish abundance.

"Un-wrappable" gifts can be extra-fun, extra-meaningful, and as a bonus, frugal as well. Coupons for services, such as babysitting (please, Santa!), house cleaning, and yard work are sure to be appreciated.

Last Christmas, I was praying a certain relative would gift us by taking our kids for the weekend, as she had done in the past. She gave me another gift, a novel, money-savvy, cool gift, but I must admit I was a little disappointed. Next Christmas, I am just going to rustle up the courage and ask her if our Christmas present can please, *please* be the wonderful, marvelous gift of the Aunt and Uncle Weekend once again.

And my mother-in-law is a master gardener. For those of you who have seen my yard, you may find this hard to believe. But have I mentioned my worm phobia? Next year, I'm going to ask dear MIL to unleash her master-gardener self on our sad yard for my Christmas gift.

Check out these "coupon-gifting" ideas from some parsimonious pals:

- Mary: "The gift of time is my favorite gift to give and receive—coupon books for various 'dates,' from free (a half-hour walk together), to movies, concerts, etc. Creating memories together is priceless. Today especially I remembered this, as it is not the material

※ ※ ※

gifts my father—today would have been his seventieth birthday—gave me that I remember, but rather the precious one of time."

- Lori: "We have zero budget for Christmas this year, and it's great how understanding the kids are with their wish lists. I'm going to make them photo calendars with tear-off coupons for friend sleepovers, their choice of a Redbox movie rental, or a Wii game rental."
- Johanna: "We are starting to make coupons a bigger part of our gift giving within our family. For example, giving a coupon for Mom to clean up a kid's room for a day, or one for a date with Dad where the kid picks the spot, or one for a special dinner cooked by Mom, featuring a favorite meal."
- Erin: "My mom gives me coupons for free house cleaning, and I absolutely love it!"
- Diana: "On the first night of Hanukkah, my husband, children, and I draw names out of a hat. And then we're responsible for providing a family member with some kind of service. Last year, Ruthie drew Micah, and she was responsible for making his bed for two weeks. She didn't mind, because he made her hot chocolate with caramel every night for the same time."

Another bonus of experiential gifts, besides not having to

wrap them? There is something to look forward to after the holidays!

LE WRAP
(A SIDEBAR WITH FRENCH FLAIR)

What's the use of saving on Christmas gifts when you're spending a mint wrapping them? This past holiday season, I spent very little money on tissue and bows from the dollar store, and wrapped nearly every gift in newspaper. Pardon *moi*? Newspaper—how gauche! But *au contraire, mon ami*. Actually, the packages turned out *tres chic*, if I do say so. I got this flower-making notion from a glossy decorating magazine, and then saw the same idea touted on a glossy decorating TV show:

- Wrap the box in newspaper.
- Cut about eight, 10″ x 10″ pieces of newsprint.
- Stack them neatly, and fold them accordion-style.
- Wrap a rubber band or piece of ribbon around the bottom of the stack.
- Round both ends of the stack with scissors.
- Open the flower by gently pulling up one layer of newspaper at a time toward the center.
- Stick a brightly colored bow in the middle.

※ ※ ※

Voilà! Your package now sports a flower that will take everyone's mind off the fact that it is wrapped in newspaper! It's even prettier with the traditional tissue-paper flowers, which you can make with leftover and used tissue.

So what do the French have to do with the Amish? Absolutely nothing. But saving beaucoup bucks on wrapping paper? That's just "Plain" chic.

Going Homegrown

Now, don't get nervous, fellow non-crafters. I would be the last person to suggest you whip up some homemade corn husk dolls for all the little girls in your family. But even I, with two left thumbs, can assemble a fun snowman kit, with a pipe, funny hat, scarf, old buttons, Oreos for eyes, and a carrot for a nose. Just add snow. Or, fill a few spray bottles with water and food coloring and call it snow spray paint. I gave snowman kits and snow spray paint to my three nephews, ages four through six, and they were a hit. I bought the hats and scarves and buttons at secondhand stores for dirt, and picked up the spray bottles at the dollar store. The most expensive element was the food coloring, which I gave to my sister-in-law separately. Only a few drops were needed to turn the water deep shades of red, green, and blue, so I'm sure one package of the food coloring lasted the entire Michigan winter. I think the whole caboodle cost five dollars a pop for a box of snowy good times.

Crafty Jill (I had her in mind when I mentioned the corn husk dolls) is all over the homegrown presents: "My kids have made gifts for the adults in the family for a few years. We have painted pottery, made candles, garden stones, and soap. It's very fun for everyone, and then I find Christmas is no longer all about their presents."

Once in a while, with variable occurrences like a monsoon or a Chinook wind, I am overcome by the desire to paint and glue. This past December, I found an old jewelry box with a hideous shellac coating and metal drawer pulls that could have matched the world's ugliest tray tables. The whole patina screamed 1991. When that mysterious crafty zephyr wafted about me, I sanded the jewelry box a little, spray painted it aqua, and glued gorgeous, multicolored enamel buttons onto the old drawer pulls. I filled it with secondhand presents, wrapped it, and put it under the tree for my daughter, Phoebe. It cost me about $12 for supplies, and a comparable jewelry box in a boutique or on etsy.com would be between $42 and $58.

Lori had a similar idea for a low-cost Christmas gift for her daughter: "I have an old desk that Anna has been wanting for her room, but I think I'm going to paint it and decoupage it a little with some dance-themed images," she said.

If you cook, can, or bake, I can bet those on your gift-giving list would be thrilled with some sort of Yuletide edible

❊ ❊ ❊

not involving green candied cherries. A friend of mine gives a made-from-scratch pie or a batch of her scrumptious home-made granola as Christmas gifts, and her recipients, including me, are enthusiastic, to put it mildly. And my sister-in-law always bakes us the most delicious bread and throws in a jar of her home-canned jam. Yum! Never once have I thought, *Gee, I wish she had gotten me a mug instead.* The pie might have cost my friend $2.50 to make; the granola would be even cheaper. Cookies cost roughly a few cents apiece to bake, and who doesn't love cookies? Somehow, there's something about a kitchen gift that's infused with so much more than the cost of ingredients. Even though the price of an apple pie or a loaf of bread or a jar of peach preserves is meager, it feels extravagant to the lucky recipient.

This is why, for next Christmas, I am saving jars of all sizes to hold some kind of "home assembled," yummy hot cocoa mix. With leftover aqua spray paint to decorate the lids, all I will have to buy is sugar, cocoa, etc.; affix a bow; and call it *Feliz Navidad*, foodie-style.

Going Secondhand

Is it tacky to buy gifts at a resale shop? I used to think so, until I gave it a spin. The Amish are huge resale shoppers (see chapter 10); they would never dream of flouncing into a store and paying full retail or even sale price on something that could be hunted down secondhand—for way less.

※ ※ ※

When I learned of the resale-shop habits of my Amish friends, I was dubious, but also intrigued. Could I really cross off a decent chunk of my shopping list at resale shops? I had been frustrated in the past, shoving countless garments in overstuffed racks apart to try and find a treasure.

> I was dubious, but also intrigued. Could I really cross off a decent chunk of my shopping list at resale shops?

But then again, that was when my thrift muscle was flabby indeed. It was time to see if the Amish were onto something.

I aimed for 20 percent of my gifts to come from resale, reuse-it, consignment, or thrift shops.

My first stop: New 2 You, a clean, airy resale shop I'd heard was fantastic from my penny-pinching friends. Phoebe loves trying on Mommy's jewelry, so I found a stylish array of costume baubles of her very own, including a darling red-beaded necklace with a strawberry pendant coin purse. Six necklaces, three bracelets, and $12 later, Phoebe had a most elegant collection to put in that used jewelry box I had redecorated for her.

I scoured Goodwill for snowman kit essentials for my nephews, and incidentally found a $55 pair of much-needed hockey pants for $5. Score!

My twelve-year-old niece received a mini-wardrobe of Abercrombie & Fitch, Gap, and American Eagle tops, plus a

✖ ✖ ✖

chunky yellow bead necklace for $20 at a hip consignment store for teens.

My favorite find of all, though, was at a new thrift shop. Well, about ten minutes into my expedition, I saw a ripped red cardboard box, half–taped shut. Not very promising looking, but still I took a closer look. Inside was a gleaming, festive Christmas plate, basically Santa's head as a platter. *Aha! My dear mother-in-law loves Santa and loves festive dishes!* I thought. Anyway, I examined it from the top of Santa's hat to the tip of his snowy beard, and it looked spanking new. Turns out, it was new. Though the box had seen better days, the plate was flawless, and the label stamped on the back said, "Fitz and Floyd." Scurrying home, I Googled "santa plate fitz and floyd," and was terribly gratified to see the exact plate selling for $25—I had paid $5.

I usually spend around $20 each for our eight nieces and nephews, so I didn't save any money, per se, on Amanda's gift. Still, I maximized the gift by buying four high-end tops and a necklace for bottom-drawer prices. She was overjoyed, too, and promptly tried on each item for me to admire (well, I made her try them on; I love a little spur-of-the-moment fashion show).

Tallying up what I would have spent compared to what I did spend made me feel like the cat who got the cream. Not counting the hockey pants, I had spent $80 less (saving $15 on the jewelry, $15 each on the snowman kits, and $20 on the Santa plate) than I would have at a retail store. Counting the hockey pants, I saved $130.

※　※　※

Do I still think shopping for gifts at a secondhand store is tacky? Not even a little bit. The thriftier, niftier me thinks it would have been perfectly tawdry to spend $130 when, clearly, I didn't have to.

> Do I still think shopping for gifts at a secondhand store is tacky? Not even a little bit.

I've also bought gifts for new babies and baby shower gifts secondhand. Those tiny ones often wear their precious wee outfits once, if at all. I recently found some fabulous boy clothes for a three-month-old—a dressy shirt, a bathing suit, and a designer T—for $5. The bathing suit still had the tags on it!

Listen to what the Elegant Thrifter, Stan Williams, had to say about secondhand gifts: "When the occasion arises to offer a gift, rummaging through my wardrobe trunk of thrift goodies usually produces results and reminds me of all the stuff I seem to have packed away without even trying" ("The Gift of Thrift: Bows upon Bows," June 4, 2010, http://elegantthrifter. blogspot.com/2010/06/gift-of-thrift-bows-upon-bows.html). His motto: "Always Frugal, Always Fabulous."

Shop Your Own Home for Gifts

As Bishop Jake would say, now we're pushing down low! What could be cheaper than wrapping an item you already

※ ※ ※

own? Talk about one person's junk being another man's treasure!

At one gathering this year, I opened up a set of super-cute Christmas dessert plates that made me ooh and aah quite sincerely. Eclectic and colorful, they were my taste exactly, and I couldn't wait to use them at my writer's group holiday soirée.

But my, my, they looked awfully familiar. Where had I seen those darling plates before?

On the ride home it clicked. Last Christmas, *I* had given them to the relative who had now given them to me! *Smart girl*, I thought of the giver, even though I didn't want to embarrass her by mentioning it. I had to giggle. The plates were spot-on for me, apparently not so much for her. I remember wishing I could keep them, and now I could—forever!

Re-gifting has an El Cheapo rap, but those plates got me thinking: if I have something in good condition that someone else would appreciate far more than I do, why in the world would I not give it to him or her?

> If I have something in good condition that someone else would appreciate far more than I do, why in the world would I not give it to him or her?

Last Christmas, Jonah, then eleven, received a hand-me-down bow and arrow set from his aunt, uncle, and teenage cousins. Bought new, it would have been way too pricey for an extended-family gift. As it was, he was ecstatic.

My friend Brian has had good luck with re-gifting: "We exchanged names with my siblings and spouses, and we all looked in our homes for something we no longer wanted," he said. "One year I gave away an espresso maker, and I got a golf bag from my brother (it was one of the best gifts I ever got!)."

Re-gifting isn't just for Christmas either. The other day, I had one of those nonstop days packed from start to finish. Oops—I almost forgot Phoebe had a birthday party to attend. There was no time to rush out and buy a gift for her pal, who, luckily, was the son of very chill, green friends of ours who are all about keeping it simple.

"Phoebe, go find Reuben some books that a three-year-old boy would like," I said. We have tons of books, and many of them are brand-new, having been sent to me by publishers and writer friends. Plus, I knew there would be lots of books that Phoebe was too old for that would be perfect for Reuben.

Of course, she came back with *The Little Girls Bible Storybook* and *Korean Cinderella*, but at least she tried. I thanked her and did a little home shopping of my own, quickly finding four or five suitable books in great shape, including a new Diego coloring book, for the birthday boy. Done—for free!

Sometimes recycled gifts can carry extra meaning for both the giver and the recipient. "For a few years when things were tight, my parents started giving away special items from our house to my brother and me," said Natalie. "They gave us artwork from our family travels, and pieces from their parents' homes. I love those gifts, because they are connection points."

Natalie's idea made me think of the home I grew up in, of items I hadn't thought about in years. Remembering things my parents displayed, such as wood carvings from Paraguay and India, gifts from missionary friends, made me feel closer to my childhood, my parents, and the "house that built me" as the country song goes.

My word—I'm tearing up just thinking about it. I'm going to call my mom and see whatever happened to some of that stuff, and drop a few hints while I'm at it. Christmas is only six months away, after all.

In our *Englisher* world, we blather on about "connecting," but the Amish are linked together in a way we can only envy. Their bond at Christmas and other gift-giving occasions has nothing to do with the exchange of expensive presents, but with spending time together and choosing small, often homemade, gifts based on need. The best things in life are free—that's a no-brainer. But obviously, sometimes the best gifts in life are free, or nearly so, too.

⌘ ⌘ ⌘

MY AMISH MONEY MAKEOVER

The Amish don't go hog wild with gift giving, but rather, they make their gift-giving occasions simple and often need based.

To Do: Think of ways you can scale back your next gift-giving occasion, especially if it's Christmas. Choose at least two people on your list and plug in some of the counterintuitive gifting options in this chapter. Let's say you select your son's teacher and your sister-in-law, whose name you picked out of the hat. I guarantee you Miss Snodgrass would rather have a batch of your famous chocolate chip muffins than another candle or ornament. And because your sister-in-law loves books, she'll be gaga for the three hardcover, cozy mysteries you picked up for her at the secondhand store—for $5 total. You've saved around $50 on what you would have spent, if you weren't a genius at seeking out sure-to-be-appreciated, alternative gifts. Hey, wait a minute, that's almost enough for a massage! What are you waiting for?

6

SAVING

Amos truly did blow me away.

Now, when you're talking about Plain folks, and you mention the name Amos, you have to clarify. (Upon mentioning to my innkeeper that I had met a charming Amish farmer named Amos, she laughed at me. "Aren't you cute!" she said, chuckling. "They are *all* named Amos.") I quickly learned that men with common names such as Levi, Jake, Eli, or Amos get nicknames to differentiate them among the populace. Hence, there is Buzzy Amos, Cookie Amos, Bald Amos, and Fat Amos ("The Amish aren't as sensitive as we are," Banker Bill explained, when I wondered if Fat Amos was okay with his ID). There's even a Dogless Amos, a man

⌗ ⌗ ⌗

who had been inordinately attached to his pup before the cherished pet died; he used to go by Dog Amos.

But back to this Amos among Amoses—he was a financial marvel. Out of all the Amish people I had talked to in three states, and I had read about many more all over the country, his money-saving story astounded me the most.

> He may be the first to save that amount while renting another guy's farm and feeding fourteen children at the same time.

At forty-five, Amos Miller, quiet, gentle, and handsome, even (a journalistic observation), had somehow saved more than $400,000 as a down payment on his own $1.3 million piece of prime Lancaster County farmland. And while he may not be the first guy in the world to save $400,000 in twenty years, he may be the first to save that amount while renting another guy's farm and feeding fourteen children at the same time.

About seven of those children were home when I visited; baby Ezra was playing with a book at my feet while his big sister Lizzie entertained him. Darling little girls in jewel-toned dresses, their hair scooped up in elegant, tiny buns, stood in a line by the sink. A toddler girl stood on a chair, dunking forks and knives into soapy water.

When I apologized for showing up during milking time, Handsome Amos good-naturedly agreed that it was not really

※ ※ ※

the best time to reveal his earth-shattering financial secrets. But he smiled shyly and sat down anyway, in one of three chairs in the farmhouse living room. I got the cushy chair.

I know already that trying to get an Amishman to toot his own horn is about as challenging as prying open a dead clam. You can call the guy fat or bald or dogless, but don't call him savvy with his money—he'll consider it prideful and shut right down. But I had to try and figure out how Amos and his sweet wife, Fern, managed to sock away a fortune while paying about $1,800 a month in rent, running a farm, and feeding and clothing their Miller multitude.

"So, Amos, I hear you just bought a farm of your own," I began.

A look of quiet pride lit up like a firefly in his eyes, then disappeared just as quickly.

"*Ja*, I was lucky enough to do that," he said.

Luck, of course, had nothing to do with it. I pressed on.

"How were you able to save that much money, while renting a farm and also raising fourteen children?" I asked. "You must have some very thrifty habits that perhaps someone like me could learn from?"

"We don't live like our forefathers did," he said, quickly deflecting any praise back a few years, like a farmhand flipping a shovelful of compost over his shoulder. "They really knew how to sit tight and save."

I knew enough by now not to butter him up, say, by mentioning that tucking away four hundred grand and plunking it down during a *national recession* is even more commendable than saving that amount in normal fiscal times.

"Have you been affected by the recession?"

"Margins are thin," he answered.

Thin margins and all, Amos saved masterfully, salting away dollars here, there, and everywhere he could find them and putting them in the bank.

In my mind, the guy's a genius, but really, saving is something the Amish do very well, almost across the board. Conserving, rather than spending, is built into the culture, said Erik Wesner. "Frugality and saving again are a cultural mode," he said. "You could surmise that this is rooted in the agricultural heritage as well. When you depend on the weather for your crops' growth and the success of your operation, you adapt to bearing the risk that they won't come through and you may have a bad year. Tucking resources away is one way of hedging for that inevitable bad year."

Dr. Donald Kraybill, the country's leading expert on all things Plain, concurred. "Saving is highly valued among the Amish," he said to me. "It's the only way to get ahead, and it's secure, not risky. Money in the bank is safe. It all goes back to a pre-industrial-Depression era, typical rural agrarian conservatism."

RAINY DAYS

"Is it gonna make down?"

That's the Amish way of saying, "Is it going to rain?"

✖ ✖ ✖

Apparently, they just plan for it to "make down," banking money against the day when it rains like crazy (for example, the economic downturn). But even if you're just having one of those inevitable bad days that we all have from time to time, socking away some funds will protect you from the "drizzle," functioning as an umbrella of sorts. Stuff happens, without fail, and it almost always costs money to deal with it.

> Socking away some funds will protect you from the "drizzle," functioning as an umbrella of sorts.

Just last week we had a soggy day, with a run of out-of-the-blue bad luck that set us back more than three hundred dollars.

First, the five-year-old accidentally stepped on the pet bird, a yappy cockatiel named Pip belonging to the nine-year-old.

You know how some people are unflappable? I am the opposite, completely flappable, especially when faced with a half-squished pet bird.

We immediately hauled off in the minivan, toting poor Pip to the vet and praying for divine intervention (I did not want to have to tell my son his bird was dead, or how he got that way). The vet did a series of tests and pronounced that Pip probably would live to squawk another day.

"We won't know for twenty-four hours if his guts are squished," he said. (He really said "guts" and "squished"!)

⊠ ⊠ ⊠

I called my husband to tell him the news. He listened patiently to my frazzled ramblings and then cleared his throat. "Uh, yeah, also, my car won't start," he said in that unflappable way for which I married him (that, and gleaming white teeth).

He dealt with *that* crisis while I was on red alert bird death watch, examining him anxiously for any signs of squished guts.

The next day, I was hugely relieved to see that Pip was upright, but something was drastically wrong with his eye. The best I could figure, it got irritated in the melee, and despite the ointment we had very bravely applied to his eye the night before (this involved capture in a towel, extreme squawking and writhing, and the deep fear I would accidentally mash the bird some more in an effort to keep him still), appeared to be much, much worse.

In fact, Pip had scratched all the feathers off the side of his face and neck, and—horrors!—there was a hole in the side of his head. *This can't end well*, I thought.

"Bring him in right away," the kind vet receptionist said. "If he doesn't stop scratching himself, we'll have to put an Elizabethan collar on him."

I zoomed to the vet for the second time in twenty-four hours, ready to pay any amount of money to just keep the bird alive. A few hours later, the office called with news. "He's doing much better," the receptionist said soothingly. "That ointment you gave him was irritating him, so he kept scratching the area."

※ ※ ※

"But what about the hole in his head?"

"That's just his ear, dear," she said.

All right, so I'm not an ornithologist.

Final cash count, for this twenty-four-hour "drizzle":

- $210 for a new car starter
- $89 for the bird's initial exam
- $10 for the blasted ointment
- $10 for eye drops for the blasted animal
- $0 to confirm our bird has an ear, likely two (the vet took mercy on my stupidity)

Just like that, $319. Luckily, we had enough money set aside to absorb the extra expenses, but we hadn't always been so prudent. In times past, if we ran into a rainy day such as this, we'd slap it on a credit card, at 16 percent interest, telling ourselves we'd pay it off when we could. Yeah, right.

But I was beginning to see the error of my ways.

Living off the Edge

"You can very easily get into trouble if you have no reserve," Bishop Ephraim, the self-taught Amish money expert, said placidly (naturally he is placid; he has a big reserve!). "Most of the Amish do not live on the edge."

Anyone who has ever lived on the edge knows the truth: it's a tense and worrisome place to be. Can I get a witness?

※ ※ ※

Without a stash of money set aside, there is nothing standing between us and very stressful times. While we may manage to muddle along the way things are now, the slightest change (a sudden spike in credit card rates, a temporary loss of income, a squished bird, etc.) could send us lurching over the edge. Besides, chugging along with no safety net, hoping nothing happens, is a nerve-racking way to live, more upsetting than we even realize sometimes.

> Anyone who has ever lived on the edge knows the truth: it's a tense and worrisome place to be. Can I get a witness?

The last time the "check engine" light came on in our van, I got a peek into my husband's psyche, and it wasn't pretty. "Whenever the cars make a weird noise or that light comes on, I get a sick feeling in my gut," he said, making a face. "Because I'm not sure how we would pay for it if something really did break down."

It was a wake-up call for me, Miss Easy-Breezy It'll-All-Work-Out-in-the-End. In the past, I would have dismissed Doyle's worries as being needless—just relax, man! But now that I was going Amish (financially), I could suddenly see his point. I also realized I had been feeling anxious about our lack of savings, and I didn't want to admit it.

I'm not alone either.

"Most people rank personal finance as their number

one stressor, usually because they feel powerless," wrote Dr. Mehmet Oz in an article for *Men's Health* magazine. "Stress not only shortens lives, it also drives people to habits like smoking, drinking, or bingeing on food. Keep some money in a special bank account, safe from your lust for a new television, and you'll establish an emotional comfort zone with major health benefits" ("Dr. Oz's 25 Health Tips to Swear By," *Men's Health*, October 2009, 154).

Wake Up Richer

The peace benefit is just one reason the bishop is a stickler for saving and encouraging the folk in his district, as well as his financial consulting customers, to put aside a good chunk of their income. "Anyone should shoot for 10 to 20 percent in savings," he said. "Pay yourself by saving."

"Paying yourself first by saving is a common trait of the Amish, and people who survived the Great Depression," said Dr. Kraybill.

I've heard that "pay yourself" line a few times before, but it never really stuck until now.

What really illuminated the whole idea for me was something I read recently that is attributed to circus guru P. T. Barnum: if you have money saved in the bank, you'll wake up richer every morning than you were the night before.

Who doesn't want to wake up richer? Talk about rise and shine! Certainly, you don't want to wake up poorer, which is

⚒ ⚒ ⚒

what happens when you have debt (see chapter 9). Evidently, our friend Amos woke up to mooing cows every morning a little bit wealthier, and that much closer to his goal of owning his own farm.

Okay, so I want to stop feeling stressed and powerless, and I love the idea of waking up a little more affluent every day. But where to start? Just where Amos started: small.

> I want to stop feeling stressed and powerless, and I love the idea of waking up a little more affluent every day. But where to start? Just where Amos started: small.

Start Small

Snag your child's piggy bank and start saving pocket change today. It's so easy to lose track of change—in your purse, your pocket, the car, the sofa. Instead, make it a point to pop in a quarter here, a nickel there, and watch your porcine savings tool fill right up. I used to keep quarters jangling around in my purse so every time the kids spied a vending machine, I could give them a quarter to buy a penny's worth of plastic junk.

But hey, I'm not Grandma, after all. And those spoiling days are gone, munchkins. There's a new sheriff in town, and she's wearing a bonnet!

⌘ ⌘ ⌘

Taking a cue from a blog on wisebread.com, I decided to use Miss Piggy as a cache of cash.

"If I had just treated my piggy bank's contents as found money, I could have had a fun evening once a month," wrote Thursday Bram in a December 29, 2008, piece called "The Piggy Bank: A Secret to Simple Saving." "But I was able to think about it as a saving tool—it was money that I would have lost if I wasn't putting it in the pig, and I worked hard to remember that fact. That money went straight into my savings account. It came in handy, too: the clunker I drove died on me one day and without my savings, I'm not really sure that I would have been able to get my car fixed."

Keep Your Eye on the Prize

"We save so we can buy a farm for our children," Sadie, a cute young mother of five (almost six), told me. 'Nuff said.

The Amish—Amos is a prime example—are stubbornly stuck on the big picture, fixated on achieving their fondest hopes and dreams; usually, this means a farm of their own or, as the entrepreneurial people shift into business, a business of their own.

For me, saving seems nebulous and intangible. How about you? Experts say it's important to give your savings account a personal meaning.

"Rather than abstractly aiming for X amount, think about why having that nest egg is important to you," wrote

MP Dunleavy in a March 25, 2009, article called "Secrets of Successful Savers," on moneycentral.msn.com. "Is it because you'll sleep better knowing your family has emergency funds? (Turns out you really will sleep better.) Is it because you can take courses that could land you a better job, leading to better opportunities for you and your kids? If saving is just about reaching a dollar amount, that's going to be hard to sustain" (2).

Quoting Angela Bauer, founder of Women in Red Savers, Dunleavy said the saving club creates that sense of meaning—and focus—by naming their savings accounts. "You may put only $10 a week into your 'new interview suit fund,' but visualizing that new suit (and maybe a new job) keeps you marching toward your goal."

Bishop Jake concurred: "If you have something to invest your money in, you'll be less likely to spend it. You'll want to save for your investment."

You Won't Miss It Either

The best—and only—way we've finally been able to start saving is by automatically transferring money from checking to savings. Believe me, if there's money in the checking account, it will probably get vacuumed up, spent on new books, clothes, pizza—even valid expenses like engine tune-ups. If the Banking Fairy, on the other hand, whisks the money away without me even remembering it's there, I don't touch it. I also don't miss it; rather, I figure out a way to make what we do have in our checking account stretch far enough.

Don't Just Save Money; Save Savings

About a year ago, I got a killer offer from a clothing store credit card, urging me to come in on a certain morning and save 50 percent on everything I could stuff into a bag, even already reduced prices. I got winter parkas for all three kids at a fraction of the cost, Christmas gifts for my nephews, clothes for Doyle and me—I was in bargain Nirvana. I totally got that rush from saving money; except, now I realize, I wasn't really *saving* any of it.

True, the kids needed coats, and I needed to buy gifts for the nephews. But I recall stuffing that bag within an inch of its life, and about a third of it was clothes I didn't really need. The deals were stupendous that day, but next time they offer that sale, I will be wiser about it, making sure anything I do buy is something I absolutely need.

I fell into a common consumer trap: the old spending-to-save drill. Dunleavy's article tells of Peter Tufano, a professor of financial management at the Harvard Business School, who did a study of people's financial habits and realized that many got good deals (e.g., "My coat was 50% off!") mixed up with saving actual money. This is messed up, says Tufano, who suggests saving your savings. For example, if your shopping receipt shows that you "saved" $67.85 on items you bought that day, go home and put $67.85 in your savings account. Now, that is a *wonderful gut* idea!

✄ ✄ ✄

A Peaceful, Easy Feeling

Handsome Amos never really told me exactly how he saved that $400,000 discussed earlier, but I know the biggest way, besides the Amish people's incomparable thrift and care with money, was his laser focus on that beautiful farm, a homestead to pass down to one of his children someday.

To be honest, I don't have a long-term saving goal I'm passionate about—yet. I do know I don't want to spend my retirement scrimping and eating cat food under a bridge, and that's only about twenty-five years away, not much longer than Amos saved for his farm.

But the more I have observed and questioned the Amish, and done my own research, the more I realized I was being foolish by not saving more. We just paid off a loan, and I'm going to have the monthly payment transferred into our savings from now on. It's a start.

Really, the most appealing part of saving money, for me, is the peace of mind that comes with it. I don't want to feel feeble and strapped, stressed out of my mind the next time some calamity befalls us.

Besides, "a dollar saved is better than a dollar earned because you are not taxed on the dollar saved," Elmer the Amishman pointed out.

It doesn't get any better than that!

⚒ ⚒ ⚒

MY AMISH MONEY MAKEOVER

"Is it gonna make down?" is the Amish way of saying, "Is it going to rain?" Apparently, the Amish just plan for it to "make down," banking money against the day when it rains like crazy (e.g., the economic downturn). Because they have a reserve, the Amish don't get all wet during drizzles big and small.

To Do: What did you do last time you had a drizzle of unexpected expenses? Think about how you can save for a rainy day, and start salting away some cash today, even if you start by plunking extra change into a piggy bank. Do try setting up an automatic transfer into a savings account. We started with $80 a month, and trust me, even that amount, piled up over a few months, saved our bacon a time or two.

7

OPERATION DE-SPOIL
THE KIDS

Freeman was wrong. It turns out, kids aren't goats (anymore), but they are money pits.

It started as we sat around his kitchen table, discussing Amish saving and sharing. Freeman is a fifty-two-year-old farmer from Michigan; he and some of his eleven children farm corn, oats, hay, and dairy replacement heifers. He sells his beef to a local ranch, a natural, no-corn-fed, no-antibiotics meat source.

"I didn't get a chance to take a shower today, so you might get a whiff of me as we're talking," he said congenially.

※ ※ ※

"Oh, you're just fine," I said, hoping that would be true.

As we settled in to the conversation, I asked him about how he's imparted that famous Amish money wisdom to his children. "How have you taught your kids the value of a dollar?"

"My goats?" he said, grinning broadly. "I haven't really taught my goats anything about money!"

Momentarily confused, I quickly recovered. "Oh, you think 'kids' are goats."

"They *used* to be!" He burst out laughing at his comic bit, and I joined him.

> How could I . . . build into my kids a piece of the same self-control, delayed gratification, and money sense the Amish form in their children?

I find it hard to believe there are people in our modern world who still think of fluffy purveyors of chèvre when they hear the word *kids*. But that's the Amish—old-fashioned and quaint (at the end of our conversation, I was relieved that I hadn't caught a "quaint" whiff of Freeman, despite his friendly warning). And it's their old-fashioned, timeworn wisdom, handed down to their little ones, that saves them countless dollars as it sets the foundation for generations to come. How could I—the modern, minivan-driving mom of three—build into my kids a piece

✖ ✖ ✖

of the same self-control, delayed gratification, and money sense the Amish form in their children? Was it possible to unravel some of the materialism and consumerism our culture—and really, Doyle and I—had wrapped them in like so much mohair?

Because a kid by any other name is still expensive, and they still want tons of stuff.

Cutting the Pie Smaller

The first time I came home from a research trip in Lancaster, having visited several Amish families, I walked into my messy house, and my three cherubs shot toward me in a frenzy of greed, wanting to know what souvenirs I had bought them.

"Whadja get me, Mom?"

I thought of Amish children I had witnessed working in their homes and farms. Amos's little daughter, Katie, about two and half, stood on a stepstool, plunging dirty forks and spoons in hot, soapy water.

I peered at my sink, overflowing with dishes.

I thought of little Moses, playing contentedly with wooden toys in a recycled ice cream bucket, and school-aged boys and girls playing games together after school and chores were all done.

My kids were rooting through my luggage like crazed baboons, looking for something shiny.

※ ※ ※

Clearly, I had failed miserably to impart either a work ethic or a sense of self-control.

Still, I knew I couldn't fairly compare myself to Amish parents, or measure my children by children raised in a drastically different culture. Well, I could, but it would only lead to me beating my head on the driveway in shame and guilt.

Besides, "when children grow up in an individualistic society, they soon accumulate in themselves a desire for more things," said Dr. Donald Kraybill, whom we met previously. "[Plain] children are not individualistic. They all dress the same, and when you grow up in a family of six to eight children, you soon learn the pie is cut into smaller pieces. The biggest thing is, Amish parents have the community to back them up when they say no to their children; you don't."

A comforting fellow altogether, Dr. Kraybill, and a wise one. Yet, I could definitely take a page or two from the Amish parenting manual. Though my children were definitely products of the "Fancy" culture in which they were raised, the junior muttons were not beyond reform. With the help of my Amish friends, Operation De-spoil the Kids was on.

Building Contentment

Who better than the mother of fourteen children to give me a North Star in one simple sentence? "It's a natural thing for children to want," Fern, wife of Amos, said softly. "We try to teach them to be content with what they have."

My kids want a lot of things—how about yours?

Just yesterday my five-year-old daughter called out from her perch in front of the fire, er, TV: "Mom, if you want that thing that squishes our blankets and jackets—like, way squishes them—you gotta call now!"

It was funny and also a little sad. She's the same cutie pie who daily begs me for:

- mail-order worms for a small-scale butterfly farmette
- "prettier dresses" for herself and her dolls, all named either "Strawberry" or "Princess"
- a pink canopy for her bed
- pink curtains
- pink furniture
- pink items of all kinds

I could go on.

She's also the same little lady who recently climbed into bed with me one Sunday morning, mournfully asking for ice cream for breakfast because "my teeth feel very warm."

That right there is the perfect example of kids wanting something and not even really knowing it's not good for them. Children *do* perpetually want things, but they can be redirected. Because the truth is, "the more children have, the more they want," or so said Atlee, a young farmer and father of seven.

How can I grow contentment in my children, and make them

*see that the things they have already are a good and cheap source
of fun?* I wondered.

I decided to take inventory of Phoebe's toys, with her help,
hopefully distracting her from the urgent need to buy worms
and wardrobe for the Strawberries.

We had a box for books and toys that we could donate to
"little girls who don't have enough special things." That box
actually filled up pretty quickly, and in the process of sorting,
Phoebe discovered some previously shunned toys that she
wanted to play with again.

The next time she beseeched me for new toys, I reminded
her of the lovely things she already had to play with. Of course,
it's not that simple to shut down a dogged young consumer
working an angle—remember, she's the one who pleaded
"warm teeth" as an excuse for morning ice cream—so I also
told her she could only ask for something new if she had played
with her current toys for an hour.

Yes, she did forget her wants by the time the hour had
passed, until the next commercial, of course. Then I told her
she could only ask for one thing a day, and to shut the TV off,
for heaven's sake.

Sigh. The Amish really do have an advantage by not having
televisions. They don't have to constantly deflect marketing
messages targeted directly at their offspring the way we do.

But I do hope my inventory experiment stretched Phoebe's
contentment muscle a little bit.

As we unearthed all kinds of forgotten dolls and games

⚔ ⚔ ⚔

and books, it reminded me of something another Amish mom told me once regarding families and thrift: "People are careful with the things they have; they try and teach their children to be careful with their things too."

Well, *yeah.* Everyone knows that, right? Except I could see with my own two eyes the dislocated game pieces, squashed books and game boxes, and toys with broken parts.

In some ways, teaching my children, especially the little one, to be satisfied with what they have started with me paying more attention to how they were treating their things. It also probably meant spending an hour or two on a scrounging mission of locating game and puzzle pieces and doll clothes and reuniting those things with their proper toys. Oh, it would be so much easier to just bag up the less-than-pristine stuff and start over with new, but what message would that send? As Andy, an Amish father of nine, told me, "A lot more is caught than taught." So hopefully, Phoebe was catching on to the fact that there were untold hours of happiness to be had playing with the things she already owned.

> Teaching my children, especially the little one, to be satisfied with what they have started with me paying more attention to how they were treating their things.

❊ ❊ ❊

97

Because, if I'm being honest, I really don't want to bring worms into my home.

A Cheaper Way

My boys are older and easier to reason with, most of the time. I'm trying to help them develop the same kind of frugal mind-set that is emerging in me after spending time with the Amish.

A biggie is filtering out wants versus needs (see chapter 10). Ezra is currently obsessed with the Percy Jackson books by Rick Riordan. At the beginning of third grade, he was a reluctant reader (the son of a writer! The grandson of a bookseller! Where, oh, where had we gone wrong?). But all that changed with Percy, and he was tearing through the series like an Angora billy mowing through a patch of alfalfa.

Do you know how easy it was for me to justify the purchase of three $7.99 books in a row? I practically threw the money at him when he asked. But then it occurred to me that those books might be available in the used section of the bookstore, so I made him look there first.

No used copies were to be found.

I could have made him wait until we had time to visit the library on the chance that the Percy installment he was on had not been checked out by seven other nine-year-old boys.

But I promise you, book four is going to have to wait.

Because as much as I deeply relate to someone becoming addicted beyond all sense to a series of books, he really didn't need it (almost); he just wanted it really badly.

Speaking of wants, parents of my generation seem to want our kids to want for nothing, except as the Amish teach us, they are desperately wanting for self-control, the ability to say no, and the capacity to distinguish between wants versus needs. The Amish are brilliant at telling the difference between a want and a need, and they transfer that discipline to their children. We need to do the same.

So, on my de–spoil mission, I had to resist the urge to coddle Ezra by immediately rushing out to buy book four. Instead, I had to do the harder work of imposing a little delayed gratification. We brainstormed about it and decided he would ask his Percy pals to find out if anyone had a copy of book four that he could borrow (he had already loaned out a couple of the books to one of his friends). Failing plan A, we would head to the library and, if need be, put his name on a list. He could also choose to spend his own money if he wanted to.

> The Amish are brilliant at telling the difference between a want and a need, and they transfer that discipline to their children. We need to do the same.

The first three books in the Percy Jackson series: $24.

※ ※ ※

The next two books: armed with a new, cheap tactic, hopefully, minus $16.

Mick Jagger and Bishop Jacob Agree

Many times it boils down to just saying the magic word: *no*.

Our kids truly are indulged, because for whatever emotional and psychological reasons (that would fill up another book), Gen X parents don't want to cause their children a moment's discomfort. And saying no to what they want is uncomfortable.

Bishop Jacob, a sage grampop of fifty-six grandchildren, some whose names he's not even sure about ("Sometimes you have to think once or twice," he admitted) gave me the bottom line: "Say no to your children, because it's *chust* not good for them if you never say no," he told me. "They'll never learn, later in life, that they can't always get what they want." (Cue the Rolling Stones, whose song "You Can't Always Get What You Want" instantly popped into my head—and didn't pop out for days.)

No to $20 worms.

Nein to $7.99 books.

Nyet to that $400 guitar, which my guitar phenom twelve-year-old really, really wants.

No. No. *No*. Because Jagger and Jacob are right. It's a tough lesson we learn continually over the course of our lives, starting, hopefully, in childhood.

✳ ✳ ✳

Sometimes no is just no. A parent doesn't need a whole song-and-dance explanation for why he or she is saying no. But, sometimes, no might mean a lesson in delayed gratification, another admirable tenet of Amish money management.

"If children want something, they are encouraged to work for it," said Mindy Starns Clark, author of several books on the Plain people, "as the Amish believe that a gift given too easily robs children of the joy of earning it themselves."

Fern said that her kids had been "begging us for a couple of years" for that trampoline I mentioned in an earlier chapter, which will probably be theirs soon. Several of Atlee's kids had been saving for over a year to go in together on a Radio Flyer wagon (the Radio Flyer #29 All-Terrain Cargo Wagon, for example, is $98 new). I visited his farm in February, and he anticipated that they would have enough saved up to buy the wagon by May or June.

Postponed bliss . . . there's nothing like it, and I have a feeling those kids will enjoy that wagon so much more because they put off buying it (under Atlee's guidance) until they could afford it.

And I think Jonah will be that much more gratified by his Epiphone Les Paul guitar, which he will buy with his own money, saved up over the course of a year. Ten dollars a pop for mowing lawns, twenty-five-dollar birthday and Christmas checks from Oma, allowance money, etc., have been piling up, and within a month he will probably have the funds in hand to buy that precious guitar.

※ ※ ※

Because like the song says, "If you try sometimes, well, you just might find you get what you need."

Too Late Schmart?

There's a Penn Dutch saying that goes, "Ve get too soon old und too late schmart."

Kids grow like clover in a hay field, and somehow in that short time, parents are called upon to impart the value of a dollar, the power of frugality, and those all-important money schmarts, er, smarts.

One brainy idea from Fern: "Keeping children busy is a good thing," she said. "They don't have idle time to think about all the things they want." And she has more than a dozen offspring to keep busy, after all.

My three youngsters may not be shucking corn and mucking stalls like their Amish counterparts, but there's plenty of work around our house to keep them prudently occupied.

Before they "get too soon old, there's a longstanding work ethic that says you're expected to work because you're part of a family," said Dr. Kraybill.

Huh. Why have I so often felt ill at ease and even guilty for putting my kids to work? It all goes back to my generation's aversion to tough love and our propensity to baby our children (I know, I know . . . another book). I mean, they do chores, but—this was made abundantly clear after I started visiting Amish homes—not nearly enough of them.

✖ ✖ ✖

I decided it would be good for my family to divide and conquer a little more, to "share the burdens" as the Plain people did.

"Work," said Erik Wesner, "is formative for children. The 'idle hands are the devil's playground' proverb is one well-known among Amish. Parents make sure to 'share' burdens with their children by having them do chores and help around the house from an early age (four or five years old is not an unusual age to already have some small tasks which you are responsible for). In this way, they are 'sharing' the cultural traits with the next generation, ones that have helped the Amish as a whole to survive and thrive."

"Thriving" has a nice ring to it.

So, thanks to Amish parents modeling their money mentoring, I launched the six-pronged "De-spoiling" plan with my kids:

1. Teach them contentment with what they already have.
2. Show them how to hunt out savings and freebies.
3. Help them distinguish between wants and needs.
4. Say no with some regularity.
5. Encourage delayed gratification.
6. Teach them that hard work won't kill them, and is probably really, really good for them.

Too late schmart? I don't think so. Hopefully, just-in-time schmart is more like it.

⚒ ⚒ ⚒

MY AMISH MONEY MAKEOVER

The Amish love their children, but they don't spoil them. Instead, they teach their little ones the value of a dollar, instilling principles of hard work and thrift from day one.

TO DO: Let's face it: all our kids are spoiled compared to Amish kids, but it is possible to "de-spoil" them in the context of our modern culture. Pick at least two categories from my six-point mission to teach my kids how to be better stewards. Next time your cherubs ask you for something, or complain about what they don't have, dig in your heels. Instead of caving to their demands, teach them a golden lesson about money and contentment. They won't like it one little bit, but then again, they don't know what's good for them, now, do they?

❊ ❊ ❊

8

REPURPOSE, RECYCLE, AND REUSE

Bishop Jake gets a gleam in his eye when he talks about the money that can be saved by finding new uses for everything under the sun—and he does mean everything.

"I'm a hound when it comes to poking around in the scrap yard," he said, grinning. We were sitting around his picnic table on the front porch of his house, a gentle spring breeze wafting around us. Jake is a cattle farmer who has a woodworking business on the side. He makes rocking chairs, clocks, desks, hutches—"whatever people want, I can make."

❌ ❌ ❌

My family wandered to the barn to look at the animals, with Jake's Chihuahua in hot pursuit. As always with my Amish friends, the vibe was totally relaxed. Although the mild-mannered bishop did get a little excited when he told me about that chicken plucker.

"Thirty-five years ago, I found a chicken plucker in the scrap yard," he said. "It would have been $500 new, and I used it for years and years."

He's passed his keenness for reusing things down to his twelve children. "My son Levi saw a house about to be torn down in Big Rapids [Michigan, a small city about half an hour from the farm]. Levi asked if he could go in there before it was torn down, and ended up coming away with a lot of good materials. With the aluminum siding and copper plumbing, he removed it and took it to the scrap yard and made $1,000. Levi removed wood and even insulation from the old house, and saved between $5,000 and $10,000 on building his own house."

I found out the Amish are habitual recyclers, even though they wouldn't think of it in those terms. "They wouldn't put out a recycling bin with cans and milk jugs, like we would," said Banker Bill. "But they would go to much greater lengths to find a way to reuse those things than we would. It's a way of being thrifty, to them."

Banker Bill makes a good point, as always: the Amish are gloriously green, but incidentally so. As Dr. Kraybill put it, "The Amish are so far behind they are ahead." They aren't plugged in, so Plain entrepreneurs must adapt equipment and harness non-electrical power sources, such as hydraulic and wind power. Amish solar heating and energy-based businesses are picking up, according to Bishop Ephraim. And farmers tend to grow their crops naturally, if not always organically, and feed their cows grass. As with everything, frugality is at the root of their avid repurposing.

Maximum reuse is their goal. Levi's project is very common. Crews of skilled Amish workers will reclaim large laminated beams before an old building is razed. They will remove and re-mill wood floors to use in their own construction projects. Even old brick and mortar from a doomed building is salvaged and used in the roadbed and under parking lots. Their mind-set is always "How can we get a second or even a third use out of this thing?" It's inspiring, really, to hear stories of Amish resourcefulness and innovation. Sometimes, it's the technological taboos—like no electricity—that encourage inventive recycling.

"A produce grower friend of mine maintains an air-conditioned, walk-in cooler on his farm, to store his produce while it is waiting to be picked up by the distributor," said Erik Wesner. "The cooler is not some high-tech model specially designed for the purpose of keeping veggies cool, but a converted semi-truck trailer, with a cooling unit rigged up inside. Does the job great—it's chilly in there! (And a welcome respite after the summer heat of picking, I can say from experience.) And I'm sure it is much cheaper than had he bought a specially made cooling unit of some sort."

My favorite story of Amish recycling? That would be from Andy, who taps his own maple syrup every year. A new maple syrup evaporator costs anywhere from $3,395 to $5,000, but Andy spent a sliver of that; while browsing junkyards, he found an old bed frame, a stainless steel tub, and pieces of corrugated steel, and cobbled them together to make a home-made evaporator. His cost: $300. "We also recycle five gallon buckets and use them for collecting sap," he told me. "You can buy them, but typically, we don't."

Darn tootin' you can buy those buckets, Andy, but they'll cost you $8.50 each! If he reuses twenty buckets, that's $170 saved. No wonder the Amish don't "typically" buy what they can simply recycle. Recycling is so much cheaper!

Now, most of the grand-scale reclaiming projects I've mentioned so far would be way out of my league—but even small recycling endeavors can pay off, like Andy and his repur-posed buckets. If the Amish can re-mill wood and reclaim *mortar*—for heaven's sake!—they can find new uses for nearly anything, and they do.

> I found out the Amish are habitual recyclers, even though they wouldn't think of it in those terms.

Mary and her family make rags out of clothes that aren't wearable anymore; sometimes they weave rugs out of the rags and sell or barter them for top dollar. Lydia cuts up her husband's old shirts and makes little ones for their tiny sons, instead of buying material. Naomi has her friend who owns a restaurant set aside empty glass gallon sweet pepper jars. "I use them for collecting milk, and they are perfect," she said. "Five-quart ice cream buckets are also ideal for leftovers, or to bring a batch of cookies over to someone's house."

Ella Yoder saves gallon apple butter cans for gardening. "I cut off the tops and the bottoms of the cans, and use them to protect the lettuce and the cabbage, like Hotkaps do."

Not being a gardener, I dashed home to Google "Hotkaps," in case my dear readers are also not possessed of the green thumb. Just as Ella alluded, Hotkaps are used to protect tender plants from bad weather, and allow the gardener to get their tomatoes or their cucumbers rooted sooner. Their motto: "Warm clothes for wimpy veggies." Their cost: $18.95 for 20.

Ella's motto: "*Free* Warm Clothes for Wimpy Veggies." Her cost: $0.

THE ARTIST SUPPLIES FORMERLY KNOWN AS GARBAGE

There's nothing better on a rainy day than a simple project that will keep the youngsters occupied while mom takes a bubble bath (now, wouldn't that be nice?). But seriously, when you've got a couple of young

Cezannes running amok, it's always prudent to have some activity on hand, especially when the DVD player is broken because someone put a waffle in it (true story). Because my ability to make crafts is somewhat limited, I look to my friends at *FamilyFun* magazine to help a girl out. So I was delighted to see their recent cover story: "Green Crafts: Recycled Projects that Cost Practically Nothing." Here are some of my favorite (even I can do them) ideas. If you like them, check out familyfun.com for instructions:

- Plastic egg cartons, watered-down glue, colored tissue paper, and aluminum wire become an exquisite (really!) bouquet of butterflies, "especially charming swaying above a houseplant."
- Bottle caps, packing tape, leftover sequins, rhinestones, beads and googly eyes, and magnets become gift-quality fridge magnets Grandma will go gaga for. (You'd pay $10 to $13 at the store for a set of six.)
- Toilet paper tubes, paint, and an old picture frame (or one picked up at the dollar store) are easily (really!) transformed into a very cute and also gift-able paper craft petal picture frame.
- Small plastic or glass jars, plain gelatin, and

✖ ✖ ✖

leftover glitter (and every parent nationwide has leftover glitter) add up to homemade, glittery hair gel. If you can make Jell-O, you can make this hair gel, I promise you! This was the hit of Phoebe's last play date, and I'm sure her pal's parents were simply overjoyed as well! But hey, it washes out, just like real hair gel.

- Medium plastic bottles (ones with a wide mouth work best), vegetable oil, food coloring, and effervescent antacid tablets (one per project!) become far-out lava lamps. Store-bought lava lamps use heat to propel the wax up through the liquid, but with these, the fizz from the antacid tablet triggers the frenetic action.

Waste Not

I'm fascinated with ways that creative people can remake stuff headed for the dump, not just into practical items, like homemade Hotkaps, but into truly beautiful, decorative, and wearable things. Companies like Maggie Bags divert countless yards of seat belt webbing, rejected by automakers for color variations, from the landfill; the result is ultrachic (and expensive) clutches, purses, backpacks, diaper bags, etc., ranging in price from $60 to $200. I totally want a seat belt tote bag, but must adhere to my newly Amish, don't-eat-the

✖ ✖ ✖

marshmallow mind-set. *Maybe someday* . . . I do have cute picture frames made from rolled-up magazines and a darling coin purse made from used pop can tabs.

Here's another example of how an Amish thrifty habit is so far out it's in, because nothing is hipper these days than garbage turned into gold. Because, as Henry David Thoreau once said, "it's not what you look at that matters, *it's what you see.*"

Reusing and reclaiming are all about developing the right vision, seeing beyond a thing's previous function to its future glory. It's also about not wasting a single scrap. "My son collects old pasteboard [cardboard] and takes it to a plant that uses it," said Ella. "He makes no money from it, but he said, 'Mamm, it's ridiculous to burn this pasteboard if someone can use it. Why would you waste it?'"

That's a good question: why do we waste so much, especially when finding another use for things could save us some money?

Check out how some frugal friends of mine in various shades of green have recycled and saved:

- Liane: "My husband is a builder so we save every piece of scrap wood we find around the yard from other projects, and throw it in the wood-burning stove in our basement to heat the house in the winter! Also, my kids and I cut up old, worn-out clothes and make outfits for Barbies, dolls, and stuffed animals—or give them to Dad for rags."

✄ ✄ ✄

- Devon: "I keep all empty containers for crafts for the kids. A big pile of fun shaped things, some glue, construction paper, stickers, and glitter and they are happy for a long time. Much better than store-bought toys!"
- Aubrey: "I have saved pieces of my kids' old clothes, blankets, etc., and I am making each of them a quilt they will receive at their high school graduations, compiled of all their own old favorite clothes."
- Tamira: "I reuse bread bags for doggy poop bags. I make blankets out of ripped jeans and save favorite T-shirts for a college quilt project for the kids."
- Linda: "I make my own breadcrumbs by freezing stale bread, buns and biscuits, and end crusts; when I have enough I bake them again until all dried out, and run it all through the food processor."
- Tabitha: "I just reuse lunch meat containers as 'Tupperware.'" (Ah, yes, the age-old margarine/ lunch meat/potato salad/fill-in-the-blank containers, appropriated by the penny-pinching into Amish/ Mennonite/Dutch/ fill-in-the-blank-with-your- parsimonious-ethnic-group-of-choice "Tupperware." A classic!)
- Erin: "I've made drapes out of a tablecloth, a dress out of a flat sheet, and a big quilted blanket out of eight of Calvin's little flannel baby blankets. It's perfect for use in the wagon or for picnics."

✄ ✄ ✄

- Natalie: "I turn legs of jeans into grocery bag holders with one hem and some elastic. And I've covered a bulletin board with the fabric from an old skirt of mine."
- Keri: "I put paper that is printed on one side back into the printer so I can use the other side."
- Catherine: "I am a HUGE fan of freecycle.org, and my fave reuse was the lady who picked up my old squishy swim noodles and used them as sword protectors!"

But wait—there's more! As much as I appreciate the reuse-it tips from these girls, it was Denise and Laurie who won the Thrifty Bonnet Award for ultimate repurposing:

- Denise: "I currently use old paper sacks and magazine pages to make greeting cards and fun stationery. I alter all kinds of jars and containers; tin cans are cute pencil holders but can also become fun little Easter baskets too. Old hardcover books that are falling apart are my favorite items to rescue, as I change them into scrapbooks and journals. The yellowing pages inside become fabulous background papers for note cards and paintings. Chipped teacups and sugar bowls have been turned into great little pots for plants, and for candle holders. A current pair of ripped-out jeans is going to be turned into pillow covers, and the back pocket will be the perfect place to keep the tooth until the tooth fairy arrives. Since I have two back pockets in good shape, I'll be able to make a pillow for each of my boys." (Tooth Fairy pillows, out of old jeans! Can you speak? Me neither.)

> Reusing and reclaiming are all about developing the right vision, seeing beyond a thing's previous function to its future glory.

- Laurie: "My mom taught me how to crochet and knit, and with all the plastic bags from Wal-Mart or any grocery stores, we cut them up into long strips and crochet them into usable bags. These are great for book bags or for using at the beach for wet or sandy beach items. I also reuse yogurt containers with lids, as they are very useful containers for fresh freezer jams." (Note: At ninety cents each for an 8-ounce freezer jam container, Laurie could save more than ten bucks if she filled a dozen saved yogurt containers.)

And Laurie's idea about making snappy tote bags out of plastic grocery bags really impressed me, as I have a major phobia about throwing out those things. I read an article once about how, not only do plastic bags take five hundred years to biodegrade, but if they end up in a waterway of some kind,

※ ※ ※

they end up choking and killing tons of birds and fish. Having a vivid imagination, I immediately had a visual snapshot of a duck being throttled to death by a bag I had carelessly tossed in the trash. Therefore I have four hundred or so plastic bags at my house. Good to know there is a way to redeem them!

Green Mama

I knew my friend Tracy Bianchi, author of the fantastic book *Green Mama*, would have lots of practical, thrifty ideas for reusing and recycling, and she totally did. Her trash-to-treasure notions:

- "One of the best things we do is take empty ketchup and condiment bottles (some lotion and shampoo bottles work too) and rinse them out and turn them into squirt guns. They squeeze and squirt way better than most at the store and don't break and leak as easily. Lots of trash turned into water war treasure!"
- "Old food containers, like sour cream or bigger food containers, we've reused to seed plants or to transfer plants and flowers we've grown to friends and neighbors."
- "Tablecloths that are stained or shrunk and don't fit anymore we've cut up to make cloth napkins, which works great, because then you don't need

paper napkins anymore. I am a lame, horrible non-sewer, so I have a friend who sews hems on them, or we just use them all frayed. Old T-shirts make good housecleaning rags. Also, old napkins or tablecloths can be stitched together to make a valance for your windows, obviously not for the best-dressed living room window, but in odd places like basements or laundry rooms, you can just take all this old fabric and turn it into a valance."

- "Old tires can be great planters; they're not super pretty, but fill them with dirt and—wow!—do they hold a lot of flowers and stuff! Used Popsicle sticks also make great markers for the garden; just take a Sharpie and write which food is planted where."

Which of these reuse-it ideas sound doable to you?

Like Devon, I save lots of things—cardboard tubes, egg cartons, glass jars, plastic jars—in our two "arts and crafts" drawers. Have you seen the price of arts-and-craft supplies and kits lately? They range from $3 for the cheap-looking, tiny wood-painting projects to $12.99 for medium-sized kits and $20–$30 for deluxe projects. Using the supplies in the drawers first forces my kids to be more creative than they would have been with a store-bought kit. The only problem is, the drawers are bulging with supplies, which poses a question: where do you store all these things you're going to reuse, reclaim, and recycle?

※ ※ ※

I finally started throwing things-to-be-reused-someday in a big box in the basement. I figure one day I'll either think of something or the recycling plant will have thought of a way to recycle it.

We've also latched onto Tracy's idea of using old dish soap squeeze bottles as water guns—big fun! And she's right: store-bought water guns pale in comparison.

I had been saving tinfoil for crafts, too, until one of my choicest blogs, myfavoriteeverything.com, came up with a more practical use: "I was a firm lover of [dryer sheets] until I found that I could take aluminum foil, ball it up, and toss it in the dryer with the wet laundry. It removes static and never has to be changed. I've been using the same aluminum foil ball for over 6 months" ("More fun laundry tips . . . assuming laundry is fun," May 19, 2010).

Dryer balls and dryer sheets both cost between six and seven dollars, but of course tinfoil rescued from lunch bags is free.

Thinking green, dryer sheets are also loaded with chemicals, and they coat our clothes with those same chemicals. How much better is it to throw a ball of repurposed tinfoil in the dryer and have it do almost the same job—albeit without the pretty fragrance—sans toxins?

Balling up the foil is a fun little "chore" to help the littlest member of your family to get involved too. In fact, once you get your family on board, everyone will be looking for ways to reuse junk of all kinds and turn it into something useful again.

※ ※ ※

Jake sure got a lot of use out of that chicken plucker, and Andy continues to churn out gallon jars of golden maple syrup from his scrap-yard maple syrup evaporator. I don't need a chicken plucker, or an evaporator, but the principle of turning junk into functional, beneficial items that save money? Now, *that* I can use.

MY AMISH MONEY MAKEOVER

The Amish are always looking for ways to reuse, reclaim, and repurpose. For them, it's not about being green, but about keeping green.

TO DO: Pick out at least three reuse-it notions from this chapter and put them into action. Once you get rolling and make a note of how much you would have paid to buy new dryer sheets, freezer jars, craft supplies, etc., you'll get in the magical mind-set of looking for new uses for everything! Warning: This gets addicting fast.

※ ※ ※

9

DEAD HORSES SMELL BAD, BUT DEBT SMELLS EVEN WORSE

The Amish may not know who Lady Gaga, Simon Cowell, or Britney Spears are, but they are up on pop-culture figures from a bygone era, such as circus maven P. T. Barnum.

What do the Amish have to do with the circus? Not much, but they do quote the man with shocking regularity on the subject of debt:

❌ ❌ ❌

Bishop Jake: "Buy now, pay later doesn't really work,"
    he said. "Making interest payments is like paying
    for a dead horse."

Ella: "Renting a farm for all those years was a dead
    horse for us."

Daniel: "It's foolish to buy something you can't
    afford, and you end up paying more for whatever
    you buy; it's like paying for a dead horse."

What is this dead horse the Amish are all fired up about?
The reference is taken from Phineaus Taylor Barnum's 1886
autobiography, *The Art of Money Getting*, in a chapter called
"Avoid Debt":

Young men starting in life should avoid running into
debt. There is scarcely anything that drags a person
down like debt. It is a slavish position to get in, yet
we find many a young man, hardly out of his "teens,"
running in debt. He meets a chum and says, "Look
at this: I have got trusted for a new suit of clothes."
He seems to look upon the clothes as so much given
to him; well, it frequently is so, but, if he succeeds in
paying and then gets trusted again, he is adopting a
habit which will keep him in poverty through life.
Debt robs a man of his self-respect, and makes him
almost despise himself. Grunting and groaning and
working for what he has eaten up or worn out, and

※ ※ ※

now when he is called upon to pay up, he has nothing to show for his money; this is properly termed "working for a *dead horse*."

Funny, P. T. Barnum was the same guy who supposedly said, "There's a sucker born every minute."

As opposed to the millions of *Englishers*—and billions of dollars—suckered into high interest debt, the Amish see frivolous credit as a plague to be avoided at all costs.

Sweet Sadie was aghast when I asked her about her views on credit cards and such: "Oh, you spend money so much more freely," she said, wide-eyed. "Your loan gets bigger and bigger, and you don't realize until it's too late how big it gets."

Naturally, thirty-year-old Sadie, who runs an organic farm with her husband and is the mother of six, has never even touched a Visa card, yet she is acutely aware of the dangers of buying things on credit. How is it the Amish got the memo about debt being dumb, and we Fancy, advanced *Englishers* are mucked up to our eyeballs in it? Again, it's a sound money habit rooted in an age-old culture.

> How is it the Amish got the memo about debt being dumb, and we Fancy, advanced *Englishers* are mucked up to our eyeballs in it?

❈ ❈ ❈

"Typically, people don't use credit cards for personal items. Historically, they use cash and checks. Why would you buy things if you don't have the money? It doesn't make sense to the Amish," said Dr. Kraybill. "Credit cards are plastic, and a symbol of modernity—it's abstract. You don't see the cash in your hand, and to them it feels like money grows on trees. That makes the Amish very uncomfortable."

It should make us uncomfortable too, but obviously, not so much.

Our current mud pit of an economy was caused, after all, by excessive borrowing and debt.

According to the Federal Reserve, total consumer credit was at $43 trillion midway through 2010. Meanwhile, a 2008 survey found that one in five credit card users have big problems paying their monthly credit card bills (what was P. T. Barnum saying about a "slavish position" to be in?). More bad news: bankruptcy filings topped 100,000 back in 2008, a 40 percent increase from 2007 (AnnaMaria Andriotis, "Ways to Reduce Debt," WalletPop.com).

I've definitely been duped into debt a time or two or three, sad to say. And I've been through the wringer with interest rates, accidentally making late payments, and also—I'm really wincing now—joining "rewards" programs.

One time I paid down a card completely and triumphantly tossed the bill when it came, except, as a parting gift, the lovely credit card company charged me a "rewards card annual fee" of $30 or some such nonsense. If you read chapter 4, you know

※ ※ ※

what happened next: I was slapped with a $39 late fee for not paying for the rewards program fee!

Insulting though it may be, I obviously hadn't had enough abuse from these chuckleheads. In the not-too-distant past, I got snookered into getting a clothing store card, baited by the promise of 10 percent off that day (WOW!); major steals—for preferred customers only, you know—in upcoming "private sales"; and yes, I'll just spit it out: a free tote bag.

So, basically, I sold my soul to the Gap for a free tote bag.

The first sale was phenomenal, although I bought a bunch of stuff I didn't really need. Hey! The deals were so great, all those little impulse buys were practically free, right? Besides, I paid the whole balance in full that month, like a good little Do-Bee.

The grateful corporation sent me a couple of $10 gift cards, which gave me warm fuzzies—what could be better than a free gift card, I ask you?

Whoever said there's no such thing as a free lunch? It was probably that quippy circus man, and he'd be spot-on. There's no such thing as a free gift card, unless you can find a way to buy something under ten dollars, with tax included. I sailed into the Mother Ship to spend my "gift cards," fully intending to use them as a $20 discount on my purchases, and never for one second planning to charge more on the card.

You know what comes next, don't you? If you don't, here's a cautionary tale for you: Upon ringing up my $50 purchase (I had already whipped out my debit card to pay the extra $30),

☒ ☒ ☒

the cashier told me I had to put the whole thing on the store credit card, or I couldn't use the gift cards.

Sighing, I complied, telling myself I would definitely pay off the $30 at the end of the month. But then, something came up that month, things were tight, and guess what? I paid the minimum balance, and unfortunately, "something came up" for the next few months, along with those gift cards.

What a chump I was! I believe the company has my photo taped up in their board room (or rather, framed in gold, with all the extra money they extorted from me), with a sign underneath it that reads, "Our Patron," or maybe "Easy Target."

Well, she's not so easy anymore, Bubba, because I now know the truth: as my role models Moses and Sadie have taught me, you can tart up that dead horse with all kinds of appealing enticements—discounts! private sales! free tote bags! gift cards!—and at the end of the day (or many, many days), a dead horse still stinks, bad.

After hopping in and out of debt like a crazy bunny for years, I finally got a grip and am now close to being debt free.

How about you? Do you have a dead horse lying around, stinking up the joint? Here's how the pros say to give that inequitable equine the heave-ho—for good:

- Stop digging that hole. Not exactly an obscure
  technique, but unfortunately, most people flop
  at this step, and never get any further with their
  debt management plan. Snip every card with some

※ ※ ※

scissors, except for your oldest card, which can be kept for emergencies (a shoe sale at Macy's isn't an emergency!). For me, what worked amazingly well was just to remove any credit cards from my purse. That simple move kept me on the straight and narrow, and ceased impulsive new charges completely.

- Pay debts off smallest to largest. This is what Dave Ramsey calls the snowball method of paying off the horse. Make minimum payments on all but the smallest amount, and throw everything you can at that one. As Frugal Dad of frugaldad.com points out in his article on getting out of credit card debt, "The psychological advantage of scoring one or two quick wins bringing balances down to zero is worth the difference in interest charges."

- Make mini payments (Ramsey calls them "Snowflakes") anytime you get your hands on a few extra bucks. Divert takings from garage sales, Craigslist, and any other source of money from your checking account—where it will get frittered; we both know that—directly to your credit card. Thirty-four bucks from the sale of that old window air-conditioning unit may not seem like much, but it will accumulate, like snowflakes do. For some reason, I didn't even know you could do this—I thought credit cards wanted their money once a month and that's the

⌗ ⌗ ⌗

end of the story. But no, it turns out you can do this, and it really adds up.

- Split minimum payments in half and pay that amount twice a month. I must admit, I didn't know you could do this either, but what a great idea! Frugaldad again, from that same article: "Interest is calculated based on the average daily balance of your account for the entire month. By making a payment every couple weeks you are reducing that average balance and therefore reducing the finance charges assessed, as opposed to waiting until the end of the month to make a single payment. As an added benefit, splitting your payment into two separate payments helps smooth out the monthly budget as you will not have to come up with an entire payment once during the month, rather half that amount twice during the month (aim for around the time you receive your paycheck)."

- Make up what you don't have. If the Amish don't have credit cards, how do they pay their bills when there's too much month at the end of the money? As Bishop Eli King said, "You gotta make up what you don't have; don't borrow it." It goes completely against the grain for the Amish to go into hock to pay their expenses. Instead, they will find extra jobs or things to sell to come up with the extra cash.

"When I was a farmer, I couldn't quite pay all my bills, so I made pallets to make up the difference,"

✖ ✖ ✖

said Andy. Ella gathers flowers from her garden in bouquets and sells them at the farmers' market for a little quick cash.

Friends of mine were scraping for the last few hundred bucks they needed to pay moving expenses and closing costs as they moved from a rented home to their own place. "Nothing is nailed down," Rudy told me, smiling sheepishly. "We sold everything we could think of at a garage sale and then on Craigslist." Moving seems to bring the "Hey, I can sell my stuff because I never use it" epiphany more than anything else. In the process of relocating from Michigan to Ohio, Dave and Jessica made two thousand bucks selling things like Dave's old guitar and other odds and ends.

Seriously, this idea could have major debt-denting potential. In this day of eBay and Craigslist, we can sell our stuff easier than ever before. Take a look at things in your house and garage with new eyes and see what you might sell for extra money. It sure beats taking on a paper route, although there's no shame in that either. Whatever it takes to stop throwing good money after bad credit card companies!

- Transfer your cards to a credit union. Suze Orman, on her blog moneymindedmoms.com, had this great little tip: "If your FICO credit score is high enough that you can land a good balance transfer deal with a credit

❊ ❊ ❊

> union credit card, go for it. Because credit unions are nonprofit, they tend to have lower interest rates and fees on their financial products, including credit cards" ("Watch Out for Sneaky Credit Card Tricks," May 27, 2010). We did this and our interest rate plummeted from 16 percent to 3 percent—fabulous! Plus, generally speaking, credit unions are more honest and upright, and they're not going to play those silly reindeer games that credit card companies play.

Remember, the Amish view debt as a very real plague, a money pestilence, a pox upon ye! They run from debt, screaming, or maybe just trotting quickly, muttering under their breath instead. On the flip side, their aversion to credit cards, said Erik Wesner, "is a big plus working in their favor."

> It goes completely against the grain for the Amish to go into hock to pay their expenses. Instead, they will find extra jobs or things to sell to come up with the extra cash.

Though P. T. Barnum came up with the dead horse analogy 125 years ago, it's no wonder the Amish latched onto it and continue to quote it often.

Here is some more old-fashioned wisdom that lines up perfectly with their no-nonsense take on life and money (P. T. had so many pithy things to say about debt, it was hard to boil them down to just two, but here are a couple of doozies to leave with you):

1. "There is no class of people in the world, who have such good memories as creditors."
2. "The creditor goes to bed at night and wakes up in the morning better off than when he retired to bed, because his interest has increased during the night, but you grow poorer while you are sleeping, for the interest is accumulating against you."

Ouch! Take heed, my friend, and we'll see you under the big top.

※ ※ ※

MY AMISH MONEY MAKEOVER

The Amish think that debt is a plague to be avoided at all costs, so they avoid all the stinky dead horse business as well, such as high interest payments, late fees, and the sickening knowledge that someone is getting richer somewhere, off of your lack of self-control!

TO DO: Resolve that debt is just as useless and gross as a dead horse, and get serious about digging yourself out of that credit hole, whatever it takes. Choose two of the debt-reduction methods listed above, and watch that pile of nonsense start to shrink.

※ ※ ※

10

SHOPPING SECONDHAND

I t was the mint green Talbots shoes that made me a
believer.

My friend Ann, a perpetual Thrifty Bonnet award
winner, and I set off with skinny wallets and fat hopes for a
day of secondhand shopping.

It was my birthday, actually, and in the interests of
researching this book, I decided to replace my usual special
shopping spree at Ann Taylor Loft, J.Jill, and Talbots (I usually cap myself off at a hundred dollars and call the spree my
present to myself) with a shopping binge of another kind.

And just as I knew that, should I ever be hiking in the
Himalayas, the wisest and most prudent thing to do would be

✖ ✖ ✖

to hire a seasoned guide named Shyam who has seen it all and lived to tell about it, there was no question that the intrepid Ann would be my fearless copilot.

Eagle-eyed and shod in sensible shoes, Ann led the way. But first, I briefed her on the fashion trends of the day. The night before, I had invested in a *People Style Watch* magazine so I could be completely up-to-date on what was in vogue for spring.

"Nautical is on-trend," I explained to her. "And mint green is a huge color for right now."

We discussed the one major ground rule: buy nothing we didn't really need, no matter how cheap it was. We would be searching mainly for women's clothing, but also for kids' and men's garb. Of course, we broke this rule a couple of times, redefining "need" as the day unspooled like a glorious, inexpensive dream.

Our first stop: New to You, a somewhat cluttered yet clean secondhand store where I had some success at Christmastime, buying Phoebe some adorable costume jewelry. Their standout feature? A "Boutique" section, with round racks of higher-end and name-brand clothing. I absolutely love this, because they do the sorting for you, and instead of getting tendonitis shoving racks of clothes aside in search of a hidden gem, you can find a treasure quickly and with much less arm strain.

Ann scoured the junior boutique rack for her teenage girls, and I swiveled through the grown-up ladies' section.

Within five minutes, I had snatched up three treasures:

⚒ ⚒ ⚒

- A Chaps Ralph Lauren pair of flannel pajamas (so cozy!): $4. Bought new: $56
- A Banana Republic long-sleeve cowl-neck top in a most flattering shade of teal: $3. Bought new: $36
- A Tommy Hilfiger T-shirt with a very sassy grapefruit motif: $3. Bought new: $22

Store #1 Tally: Chaps pj's, a Banana top, and a Tommy Hilfiger tee, all for $10. May I repeat? $10. This was getting good, and Ann and I had just begun.

Stan Williams from the swank-on-the-cheap blog elegantthrifter.com clues us in as to why garments like these are selling at such slashed prices: "It's like new cars," he said. "The second they leave the showroom, their value drops 60%." Hey, I wasn't going to argue with the prices, just fork over $10 fast and make a mad dash for the door.

Our next stop: Worldwide Thrift and Gift (store #2), also clean (a big deal to me, because a musty smell is a major love-buster!) and, as opposed to lots of secondhand stores, spacious and wide-open.

My finds:

- A South Pole mint green and white–striped, short-sleeved rugby shirt for Jonah, sized 12–14: $3. Bought new: $17.99
- A chunky bead necklace: $3. Bought new (although I couldn't find the exact necklace online, I did find

※ ※ ※

quite a few comparable pieces; this was also a fashion fad I had ID'd from the magazine): $15

- A mini cable-knit black cardigan with three-quarter sleeves: $2. Bought new: $12 and up. There was nothing trendy about this sweater, which made it even a better find in some ways. A classic piece like this can and does go with everything.

Yeehaw!

Store #2 Tally: A dressy polo for Jonah, a necklace with style, and a versatile classic sweater to go with trendier pieces, for $8.

Feeling smug indeed, Ann and I figured we would make one more stop; anything we might find at Goodwill (store #3) would be icing on the cake at that point.

What we didn't know yet was that we would find the pièce de résistance, the bargain of the year,

> Bought new, the nine items I bought at the thrift stores would have cost me a king-sized $237.48. That's a $211.98 bundle saved, folks. Not bad for a three-store foray into frugality, is it?

whereof the Thrifty Bonnet winner would get choked up and thank her parents, her agent, and the store where it was obtained.

❊ ❊ ❊

I'm talking about the shoes that morphed a pay-full-sticker-price gal into a secondhand believer.

Ann spied them, naturally.

"Lorilee, did you see those mint green shoes over there?"

I have to confess, I rarely check out the shoe racks at secondhand stores. Indeed, the pickings can be slim. But not on this fine day.

They were the color of chalky wedding mints in little netted bags, suede ballet flats with a tiny bow at the top of each shoe. They were in mint condition, if you will, just shy of brand-new.

Trying them on was a Cinderella moment, but the best part came an hour or two later, when I Googled the shoes. Wonder of wonders, they were *currently being sold* at Talbots. For $48.99. I could cry for joy when I tell you I paid $3 for those irresistible shoes.

My Goodwill take also included:

- Eddie Bauer men's socks, in the package: $1.50. Bought new: $7.50
- House of Blues T-shirt for Ezra: $3. Bought new: $22.

Store #3 Tally: Brand-new socks for Doyle, an ultracool tee for Ez, in perfect condition, and—be still, my clotheshorse heart!—stupendously cute, mint green shoes for me, at the Lilliputian price of $3.00. Total: $7.50.

Total Day's Tally: Designer 'jams, two designer tops,

※ ※ ※

one pair of nearly new on-trend shoes, a basic cardigan, and a chunky bead necklace for me; a name-brand dress shirt for Jonah; two pairs of dress socks for Doyle; and a stinkin' hip tee for Ez: $25.50.

Bought new (and everything but the pj's were in pristine condition; they were a little nubby) these nine items would have cost me a king-sized $237.48. That's a $211.98 bundle saved, folks. Not bad for a three-store foray into frugality, is it? The only item I kind of regret is the Banana Republic top. On the rack, it looked flattering, but since the store was about to close I didn't have time to try it on—a beginner's mistake.

But better a $3 gaffe than a $30 one, any day.

AN EPIPHANY IN KATIE'S KITCHEN

In Katie's kitchen, with the intoxicating aroma of toasting oats, cinnamon, sugar raisins, and nuts all around us like a sweet dream, I first caught the resale vision.

She and her daughter Martha were rolling out dough for half-moon pies while homemade granola baked in the oven. As usual, I sat while the Amish baked, inhaling good smells and good money wisdom at the same time.

A paper crafted heart, framed by Popsicle sticks, dangled over the spotless sink. A picture of a bluebird was at its center, with the words *Gott ist die Liebe* arcing over the top. Instantly, the old Mennonite hymn began to play in my head, and that music, coupled with the baking smells and the gentle

❌ ❌ ❌

surroundings of the farmhouse took me to my grandma's farm, where I learned that *Gott ist die Liebe*—God is Love—in so many ways.

Katie, according to her husband, Andy, loves garage sales and resale shops.

"I've gotten lots of good things there," she said, "games and puzzles and books for the children, for gifts."

Her biggest resale bargain is probably silverware sets, complete with six to eight place settings. When her daughters got married, Katie sent them to their wedded lives with some basics to set up housekeeping. "I spent between three and five dollars on those sets," she said. "It was a good buy."

Ja, it was a good buy, Katie—it was a fantastic buy.

When I got married, I registered for silverware—or "cutlery," as we Canadians called it. My mom's friends had a shower for me, specifically to fulfill my wish for fancy flatware. The cold meat fork alone was eighteen dollars. However, it was a most enchanting cold meat fork, of which I am most fond. I still don't know exactly what to do with it, but I sure am fond of it.

That afternoon in Katie's sunlit kitchen, I had an electric lightbulb moment: shopping resale could save me tons of moolah.

Oh, I had dabbled, to be sure. I was an especially big fan of children's consignment shops, where I had picked up loads of designer or name-brand (Abercrombie & Fitch, Ralph Lauren, Gap, Talbots Kids; even the faboo Euro brand Oilily) duds for the kiddies. And I am like a pig wallowing in mud

❊ ❊ ❊

when I scout out a garage sale with heaps and heaps of splendid books.

But I rarely bought clothes for myself secondhand, and had never thought of thrift stores as a place for furniture, dishes, and silverware, or gifts.

I left Katie's farmhouse with a warm, oozy apple half-moon pie in hand, and a new outlook on shopping. If she could find an eight-piece place setting of silverware for her daughter for five dollars, chances were good I, too, could score like Wayne Gretzky on a tear, if only I would open myself up to the possibilities.

In Abigail's kitchen, all doubt was banished.

The mother of seven and grandmother of five, Abigail is a huge proponent of secondhand stores. "I buy bedding, towels, dishes, glass tumblers, shirts for my husband," she said. "One time, I found a Trivial Pursuit game in good condition, with all the pieces, for a couple of dollars." (That very game is the centerpiece of the now-famous Amish Trivial Pursuit nights, which I heard about from Banker Bill and to which I was eventually invited for an outstanding evening! See the final chapter for more nitty-gritty details.)

Abigail also collects pottery in the McCoy Brown Drip style. She hunts them out at secondhand stores, and once even got a piece of the real McCoy, displayed appealingly in her Amish-crafted wooden hutch.

Turns out, shopping secondhand is a major money secret of the Plain. Almost every Amish man or woman I interviewed mentioned garage sales and "reuse-it" shops as their main sources of bedding, linens, socks, baby Onesies and pajamas (though not, Sadie said with a giggle, "anything with Batman on it"), games, books, dishes, and kitchen tools. Coats and shirts are "made over to our standards," said Atlee. "It's cheaper than buying material."

> As the quotable Ella Yoder said, "You don't have to buy something new to buy something good."

And for a supremely modest subculture, the Amish freely shared with me all about their underwear, or at least where they buy it: at the thrift shop!

My old thinking: *Ewww.* My new thinking: *Enough hot water and bleach will get those pantaloons good as new.*

On the topic of underwear, did you know the Amish call bras "*diddy hosen*"? If you translate from the German, as I did, you'll get a good chuckle. Let's just say "hosen" is "pants," and leave it there.

The quotable Ella Yoder said, "You don't have to buy something new to buy something good." Well said, Ella. Listen to the good things these Fancy friends of mine procured, at massive discounts:

- Kris: "My neighbor just told me she bought a high-end $3,400 bike that was used four times for $200 at a garage sale. I'd say that's a pretty good deal!"

✳ ✳ ✳

- Rachel: "I bought six solid-wood bar stools at a garage sale for $75. I had been shopping for bar stools for months, hoping to catch a deal, and I know that the ones that I got were worth from $800 to $900. I actually felt a little drunk afterward, I was so happy."
- Elaine: "A man's cashmere sweater at Goodwill for $5. It's the high-quality cashmere too. It even holds up to being machine washed (on gentle)! It's a pretty bright blue that is good for my blond husband."
- Dave: "I have a pair of very rock 'n' roll True Religion jeans I got for $6 at Goodwill that sell at Nordstrom for $198. PAKOW!" (Dave likes to make these sci-fi shooting/disco noises to emphasize his point.)
- Jessica: "A new, with tags on, silk shirt from Express for $4.99 that was originally $50. I've also found at thrift stores numerous Ann Taylor and Banana Republic clothes that are barely worn."
- Natalie: "I got a gorgeous, full-length, black, men's cashmere winter coat for $2 at Toronto's famous bargain event, the Hadassah Bazaar."
- Dana: "I got a pair of Express jeans at Salvation Army (on Wednesday, which is half-off day), that I later discovered had a broken zipper. Express has a lifetime guarantee on their clothing, so after calling the store to make sure it was okay, I exchanged them for a *brand-new* pair."
- Sarah: "My favorite thrift store is a gem near

✕ ✕ ✕

Sewickley, Pennsylvania—a town where there is lots
of old money and ladies who like to shop often and get
bored with their selections. I regularly get brand-new,
name-brand clothing—often with tags still attached—
for less than $5. My favorite, though, was a brand-new
J.Crew dress for $2.99 (it was half price) that I still
often wear to weddings and special occasions!"

- Denise: "At the Salvation Army, I got a vintage wool
  coat with mink collar for $5.00, and at a garage sale I
  found my very first dining set: a table with four chairs
  for $20.00 in perfect condition. That was a number of
  years ago, of course, but a total bargain nonetheless."

- Keri: "I took my son to Goodwill, where he found a
  pair of American Eagle khaki shorts, which would retail
  for about $40 to $50; we bought them for $1.99. It gets
  better: the first time he wore them, he found $50 in the
  pocket! Best deal ever!"

- Tracey: "I once nabbed an armload of brand-new
  Hannah Anderson and GapKids outfits for $8. I don't
  know what the deal was, but a huge gazillion-dollar
  house was having a garage sale, and she had bins of
  clothing. Barely or never worn, tags still on. I grabbed
  boutique brands and high-end clothes by the armful
  and paid $8! A most triumphant day. Only thing that
  tops that sale was the awesome Big Wheel we garbage
  picked and still use."

- Julie: "I bought my dining room table at a garage sale

⚹ ⚹ ⚹

in Kansas City. It was in a dark corner of the garage when I spotted it. I had been looking for a large farm table for six years, but couldn't find one priced under $5,000.00. They were asking $150.00, and I asked, with the horror of my husband, if they'd take $125.00! They did! It wobbles, but other than that, it is in perfect condition and had eight leaves that came with it. So c'mon over for dinner!"

These testimonials bear out Ella's Amish wisdom on the topic. You certainly don't need to buy a new bike, or jeans, bar stools, designer clothes, a farm table, or anything else we've already mentioned to "get something good." I love all of these thrifty stories, but my favorite has to be Keri and the American Eagle shorts with $50 in the pockets. Bonus!

Speaking of unexpected windfalls, the craziest tale I ever heard of thrift store madness was the 2.6-carat diamond ring, set in platinum, found in a Harrisburg, Pennsylvania, Goodwill in 2010. It was appraised at $17,000 and sold to support Goodwill charities!

A Bird in the Hand . . .

Turns out, Ann and I were misguided in our firm resolve not to buy anything we didn't absolutely need. Frugal guru Ms. Shopping Golightly, on her Thrifty Chicks blog (http://thethriftychicks.blogspot.com), advises shoppers to go to resale establishments without a list in hand. Her reason: if you're looking for just, say, khaki men's pants, size 38/32, for example, you'll be disappointed and empty-handed when you leave. But when you keep your mind open to any possibility, it's then you'll spot real goodies, such as these gifts she found months ahead of time for her friends (from "Thrift Store Tips #1: Converting the retail mind to the Zen of Thrift," June 25, 2009):

1. "A French Madeline baking tray for $2.99 that was $35 on sale at the local gourmet store. My best friend loves Madelines. They remind her of a train ride to Versailles on a cold, rainy day. She also loves to bake. So what if her birthday is six months away? Buy that tray and save the $32."

2. "An original, hand painted Dutch oven. It's vintage and in great condition. I can almost smell the things that have roasted in this treasure and I have a friend who can make this oven waft smells that will make his neighborhood salivate with scents of lamb, pork, brisket. It's $4.99, I already know it's something ridiculous on eBay and what would be the cost of shipping this hunk of iron?"

You see, a bird in the hand—and the Madeleine tray and Dutch oven were definitely "birds"—is different from accumulating a bunch of stuff that catches your eye, but that you will likely never use. The wisdom comes in knowing the difference.

If you spy something you know your mother-in-law will love for Christmas, or a book your husband has been waiting for the paperback version to buy, nab it now, even if it's not something hugely practical for this blessed minute in time and space.

Tips on Buying Used Clothing

1. Rethink it. Some folks won't buy used clothing because they think it's gross that other people have worn it. This might be true, but only if you don't have a washing machine (or an Amish washboard and plenty of hot, soapy water). Remember, even if you buy a pair of $200 pants at a top-drawer boutique, chances are astronomically good that a few people have tried on the same pants. What's really gross? Retail prices.

2. Mix and match. Jill Wallace, the vice-president for community relations of Goodwill of Greater Grand Rapids, said the style-conscious should mix it up: "Being a fashionista is hard enough, but being fashionable on a budget is somewhat of an oxymoron to those who have not shopped at Goodwill. My favorite tip for the Goodwill shopper is to pair something new with something gently used. Anyone can pull this off and save at least 50 percent on a name-brand ensemble. It's

※ ※ ※

all about the search. You can't go into a secondhand store looking for something specific. You need to keep an open mind. Dig for those labels that you find at the high-end department stores. Once you have found something, imagine it paired with pricey jeans, the shoes that you just couldn't live without, or the mini that you know will only work for another year (that you may or may not have purchased on sale). The end result . . . you be the judge."

3. Try things on. It's not a great buy if it makes your body look weird. I'm just saying. The thrift stores I frequent have nice, clean dressing rooms, so there is no reason not to quickly try on that $3 top from Ann Taylor Loft.

4. Don't buy clothes you won't wear. Okay, so that sweater from Anthropologie is $7, and you've never owned a sweater from Anthropologie. But the buttons are shaped like ducks or something, and it's a bit odd. You have nothing to go with it. What are you thinking? Again, it's no bargain if you won't get use out of it. What it is, my friend, is $7 floating down the River Silly.

5. Don't limit yourself to favorite brands. It may be comforting to find old favorites, but once you develop that Thrifty Bonnet eye, you'll find wonderful pieces from brands you've never heard of.

6. Think accessories. Like my chunky bead necklace,

❋ ❋ ❋

there are oodles of accessories—jewelry, belts, handbags—available at thrift stores. A friend of mine was recently spotted slinging a totally trendy, lavender bag that looked exactly like one I had seen in a clothing store flier. "I got it at this secondhand store in [a wealthy part of Grand Rapids]," she said, all twinkly eyed. What? But then again, why should I be surprised?

7. Brief yourself on what's vogue. The mint green shoes are my best example of checking out the trends before you hit the resale shops. Had I not seen the mint green trend in *People Style Watch*, Ann would have sailed on by the best fashion find of the year. If you don't want to spring for a magazine, be sure and peruse the department store fliers, or Google "fall fashion trends" or whatever season you're in. Bonus: It's great fun to discover something faddish yet fabulous for dirt. Even if next year the craze is over, if you spend $4—oh well. It was fun while it lasted.

> A bird in the hand is different from accumulating a bunch of stuff that catches your eye, but that you will likely never use.

8. Because it's good for the soul, institute a "one in, one out policy." Every time you bring home something new, get rid of something old. Give it away, throw it in the thrift store box—just take it out of circulation. This

✳ ✳ ✳

has been a marvelous idea for me, because I tended, in the past, to buy too much at garage sales or my favorite children's clothing consignment shop. It was cheap, but it led to just too much stuff to deal with. Now when I shop, I think, *If I buy this shirt for Jonah, which one goes in the box?* It tends to balance things out nicely. Or, do what Christine does: "My annual clothing budget is $0. Once each season, I take about a fourth of my clothes for that season to the consignment store. With the cash, I purchase one new outfit for that season. Oh, that $0 includes shoes, purses, and jewelry! My husband is delighted."

9. Define your "upper limit." What is your "upper limit"? Ms. Shopping Golightly calls it her "flinch point," the amount—in her case $5—where she forces herself to do some soul-searching. *Is it worth it? Can I really use it? Can I live without it?* This helps her pare down her purchases and not spend too much. "Do you have a flinch point on items in the thrift market?" she asks. "In the new goods market? Or do you just spend with no inhibition? If so, the retail market flings an invisible pie in your face every time you make a purchase and you aren't even aware enough to see what flavor it is. I prefer Banana, but not in my face" ("What's Your Flinch Point," Thrifty Chicks blog, February 8, 2009). We prefer shoofly, Miss Golightly, but we do get your point.

※ ※ ※

Tips on Buying Furniture and Home Décor

1. Debrief yourself with a great flea market magazine. Just as *Style Watch* guided me in what fashions to look for, *Flea Market Style* gave me tons of super creative ideas from seasoned flea market finders with much more experience and imagination than I have. One issue gave me tips on what to do with old tablecloths, crocheted odds and ends, funnels, and old Reader's Digest Condensed Books. This last one was a godsend; since my late, great dad gave me these books, I was loath to throw them away. Now, when that intermittent, hot-glue-gun gust hits me, I can make place mats, a pendant, or even fruit cones that have to be seen to be believed. I consider myself a reasonably creative gal, but I have never once looked at those dusty, precious books and thought, *Fruit cones.* Studying a magazine like this, or a blog such as www.restyledhome.ca, will give you new eyes to see all the wondrous possibilities for your home in the thrift store.

2. Think *Junque.* Stan Williams, the "elegant thrifter," does thrifting as high art; he mixes serious antiques with what he calls "junque." Again, it's rethinking how and where you're going to decorate and furnish your home. Stan said, "Vintage style adds instant heritage to any room . . . When decorating with vintage objects, we're able to express our individuality and our

creativity can thrive when we are on limited budgets" ("Design Sleuths," *Flea Market Style*, 2010, 26).

3. Buy only what you love. Once the thrifting bug bites, you might get lightheaded at all the sensational steals. After all, experts say home décor and furniture resells at an average one-tenth of original cost. Wow! Wooziness leads to forking over $200 for a leather chair from Pottery Barn, and let's be real: you've never been fond of leather furniture. Here's an easy test: if something calls to you from across the store, and your pulse races, and your mouth goes dry, you probably love it. Or, just ask yourself, "Do I love this, or just like it?" True love stands the test of time.

> Because it's good for the soul, institute a "one in, one out policy." Every time you bring home something new, get rid of something old.

4. Buy only what you need. Wait a minute, there, Amish wannabe. Didn't you just say, "Oh, if you find an early anniversary gift for Aunt Irene and Uncle Floyd, by all means, even if you don't technically need it, buy it!"? Yes, I did. And I stand by it, if we're talking about smaller purchases, like a decorative planter or a breakfast tray you know will make a great, personalized, and meaningful gift for someone. But if we're talking furniture,

※ ※ ※

it's stupid and senseless to buy something you don't really need, but simply catches your eye. Of course, if you can think of an honest utility for the piece, and it won't just sit in your garage, go for it. Take an inventory of what kinds of pieces of furniture you truly need around the house. We need bookshelves for my office, the sunroom, and Ezra's room, a great piece to hold our TV and DVD player, and chests for both Phoebe and Jonah. We don't need another china cabinet, but that's what I always end up staring at for ten minutes anyway.

5. Buyer beware. Even if you love it or need it, there are a few good guidelines to follow when purchasing used furniture. Linsey Knerl of The Dealista offers the following prudence:

- Buy solid hardwoods, such as maple or oak; otherwise, she said, "it won't stand the test of time. Some furniture was never built for more than one owner."
- Look for quality construction: "Check underneath the seats of chairs for corner blocking that is not only glued but bolted for extra support."
- Does it smell funny? If it's an upholstered item, say buh-bye, no matter how cute it is. That funky tang ain't never leaving. With wooden armoires and chests, though, there's hope. "Leave drawers in the sun for an afternoon. That will open wood's pores

✖ ✖ ✖

and release odors. Indoors, try baking soda in a salad plate to absorb odors."

- Open drawers, sit on the chairs, lean on a table, and watch for creaking, moaning, or wobbling, telltale sounds that warn you should reject the piece. But, if after all that, it feels stable and solid, it usually is.

- Consider original use, sometimes. It's okay to pile an antique china hutch with towels and linens or books, but not electronics. "These pieces don't have adequate ventilation for products that generate a lot of heat," she said. "It could be a fire hazard." (Linsey Knerl, "Your Guide to Buying Second Hand Furniture," The Dealista, March 2010)

Tips on Garage Sales

You never know when you're going to come across a driveway heaving with garage sale wonders. Hmmm. *Heaving?* An odd choice of words, you might say. But when you consider that many people are purging the contents of their homes of bulk items and buy one, get one free "deals" they never used, it fits the bill.

And sometimes purveyors of garage sales just want to get rid of stuff, even if they know full well they could sell it for way more on eBay or Craigslist. Julie's $125 farm table, Kris's friend's $200 bike, and Rachel's $75 bar stools are great examples of the kinds of killer bargains to be had in your neighbor's

✖ ✖ ✖

yard. Last year, Doyle, who hates garage sales (and shopping of any kind), saw a snowblower for sale at someone's yard sale and stopped to check it out. He left with a $50 snowblower (bought new, it would have been between $300 and $600), and the thing worked like a charm all winter long.

Of course, garage sales are completely hit-and-miss. You can go to ten sales and look at a lot of plastic flowers and doilies, and the eleventh one has Gymboree clothes in your kids' sizes, hardcover books by your favorite authors, and a Pottery Barn coffee table that reduces you to tears.

That does happen once in a blue moon, happily. Plus, it's just fun to look at other people's stuff sometimes; am I right? I do find that I get very birdbrainish at garage sales, flapping around, getting excited, and ending up buying something shiny I don't need. It does feel weird leaving empty-handed, especially when it's you and the seller, alone, and there's this awkward moment when you know and she knows there is nothing appealing to you whatsoever among the items she has worked so hard to sort and label. I tend to feel bad for the person and her crowded driveway of junk, and feel compelled to buy something out of pure sympathy.

I know, I know. Grow a spine, lady.

And while I'm growing one, here are a few more tips for successful garage saleing:

- The early bird gets the worm. This is bad news for night owls, but good news for you perky early birds.

※ ※ ※

Go ahead; pick it over. I'll be along in a couple of hours to get your leavings.

- Or does she? It feels kind of rude, at first (for a Mennonite girl like me, anyway), but you can haggle, or "higgle," as my thesaurus suggested. Do keep in mind that you may be able to get the seller to go lower. Try bundling two or three items and quoting the seller a discounted price for the lot. Remember, they want to purge, so they may jump at the chance to get rid of a few items for a few less bucks, especially if it's getting later in the day (take that, you chirping chickadees, up at 6 a.m., all smiley and happy!). So, haggle or higgle, it doesn't hurt to try.

- Peer deeply. Just like Julie, who spotted the deal of the century, that $125 farmhouse table, in a dark corner of someone's garage, be sure to poke around the murky nooks and crannies for semi-hidden gold. Not only will you be doing a thorough search for good stuff, but if you score, you'll also have a great story. "It was a dark and stormy night, and I was about to leave, when I decided to see what that beautiful piece of woodwork was, over by the guillotine, obscured though it was by eight inches of cobwebs. And grime. And dried blood."

Let's say it all together now: "You don't have to buy something new to buy something good."

※ ※ ※

I'd love to chat some more about this, but it's a Friday in June, and this newly converted resale maven's got some garage sales to go to. Happy thrifting!

※ ※ ※

MY AMISH MONEY MAKEOVER

The Amish wouldn't dream of paying retail, and they save tons of money by hunting down screaming deals at thrift/secondhand stores, consignment shops, and garage sales.

TO DO: Make a list of clothes, housewares, and furniture you need at your house. For example, my list would include boy's clothes in sizes 9 and 12, men's dress shirts (I just snagged an Eddie Bauer flannel in great shape for Doyle), girl's size 6, and women's size . . . (Now, that would be telling.) I would add to my list: drinking glasses, a bed dust ruffle, little girl's twin-size bedding, decorative canisters and boxes to "wrap" presents in, bookshelves, and chests for Jonah's and Phoebe's rooms. Google resale shops in your area (often there are star ratings and user reviews), and pick three you want to check out. March forward, armed with your list, an open mind, and the knowledge that you don't have to buy something new to buy something good!

✖ ✖ ✖

11

TO BULK OR NOT TO BULK?

Ella Yoder is making a batch of snitz pies.

I had never heard of snitz pie, so I thought she was saying "six" pies. "My daughter-in-law is having church at their house tomorrow, so I thought I'd help her out and make some pies," she said cheerfully, as she opened gallon tins of apple butter and poured them into a huge stainless steel bucket on her kitchen floor.

"Wow!" I said, sitting, as usual, as an Amish lady buzzed around the kitchen like a worker bee. "Six pies!"

"Oh no," she said, stopping momentarily from her task of adding tapioca to the bucket. "It's not six pies. It's *snitz* pies, ya know, probably about fifteen of them."

If I made six pies, the local media would be alerted. If I made fifteen pies, CNN would be alerted.

"Oh," I said, overwhelmed by the thought of making fifteen pies. Luckily, the talented Ella was making them, not me. "So then, what goes into a snitz pie?"

"Dried apples, apple butter, applesauce, tapioca, sugar . . ." She continued listing the ingredients. "It's cheaper to make a lot at one time—much cheaper. And we buy in bulk once a month. There's a huge difference in price when you buy in bulk."

Snitz pie, I learned, is a special treat for eating after Sunday services. Ella purchases flour 100 pounds at a time, and sugar 50 pounds at a time. She buys gallon tins of apple butter, though she does make her own applesauce. The dried apples, though, are a sore spot. "Years ago," Ella said with a *tsk*, "I would dry my own apples for snitz pie."

Clearly, Ella believes she is slacking off in the dried-apples department (I don't have the heart to mention the huge tins of apple butter), but she's still getting a good deal buying in quantity. (Dried apples are $7.79 per pound bulk, and $18.00 per pound at the grocery store.)

BANANAS FOR BULK

The Amish are bananas for bulk, and of course, most of the reason why is rooted in their penny-pinching ways. "They buy in bulk quantities at dry goods stores or damaged goods

✖ ✖ ✖

outlets (these are typical in Amish communities) where you can get damaged-package goods, or near- or past-the-expiration-date products that are still perfectly good, at a deep discount," said Erik Wesner. "Wal-Mart is another mainstay in many settlements, and you might have a weekly or monthly trip where a van will pick up a number of Amish housewives in an area, and they split the cost of the ride to the store and knock out a huge grocery purchase at one time."

Nearly every Amish community has a bulk foods store of their own, and, as Erik pointed out, even Wal-Mart is a monthly destination for Plain shoppers, as is Sam's Club and Costco.

"Not having the vehicle at hand really cuts down on frivolous travel, and it forces you to plan ahead, and do things like buy in bulk quantities," he said. "I wonder how much unnecessary gas and money we burn running to the gas station for a late-night overpriced gallon of milk. I've certainly taken that trip."

Unfortunately, I am the *queen* of taking that trip, more than once a week, dashing out the door for a milk run, or for school snacks or bread or something else of which I've run out. I definitely am "paying through the nose," as my dad used to always say, for the convenience of a last-minute grab 'n' go.

What would be so much more expedient, mind you, would be if I actually stockpiled some of this stuff so I wouldn't run out at 10:30 p.m. I only have so much room in

⋇ ⋇ ⋇

the fridge, so milk is probably something we will always run out of. But school snacks? That I could buy in bulk. Katie does.

"I get peanuts, roasted sunflower seeds, sesame sticks, and raisins at the bulk food store, and then I mix them up and make snacks," she said, with the serenity of one who does not have to face snackless children on crazy school mornings.

Amish homemakers buy things like snacking supplies, candy, and baking ingredients in quantity and resize them in smaller measures. For example, 100 pounds of rice gets resized into 10-pound bags. (I always run out of rice, come to think of it. Hmmm . . .)

Actually, the Amish buy everything possible in bulk. "Let me think about it a minute," Bishop Jake mumbled, stroking his beard thoughtfully. "Well, for our planting, we buy seeds in bulk, and plastic for mulch, and for cooking and baking, we buy sugar in 50-pound bags."

"Flour?" I prompted.

"Oh no," he said. "We grind our own flour from speltz; it's easier for your body to assimilate. And then we sell whatever we don't use locally."

Speltz? Now, this would require a Google. It's actually spelled "spelt," although the Amish commonly call it "speltz." It's a relative of wheat, and a staple peasant food mentioned in the Bible, the ancient writings of Horace, and the poetry of Pushkin. Naturally, the Amish are all over it.

※ ※ ※

"We buy salt in a coarse form and grind it ourselves too," said Bishop Jake, getting warmed up. "It's cheaper than buying salt at the store."

Although I am a Mennonite wheat farmer's granddaughter, I don't think you're going to catch me grinding my own flour or salt anytime soon. However, it was time for me to investigate this Amish money habit—buying in bulk—to see if it would also save me some cash.

Truthfully, I had my doubts.

I only have three children, after all—not fourteen, like Amos and Fern (the average Amish family has seven children). A big part of Plain folk buying in bulk is driven by their bulk-sized families.

> The Amish are bananas for bulk, and of course, most of the reason why is rooted in their penny-pinching ways.

I had also heard cautionary tales from friends who had been burned by bulk; instead of saving their money, they had actually paid for something they never used.

"It's so exciting at first; you get such a rush from all the deals," said Torey. "But then you discover too late that, yes, you might like olives, but you might not like a 40-ounce jar of olives. And there's nothing worse than realizing you have ten more pounds of tortellini, and they don't let you sell tortellini on Craigslist."

Yet, Torey, yet.

⌗ ⌗ ⌗

Curious about bulk shopping, I embarked on an exploratory field trip to compare prices between the local warehouse club and my local grocery store. First, I scanned our cupboards, fridge, and freezer for foodstuffs we actually needed, because need is key. Knowing how flighty I can get around sales, and having heard stories like Torey's, I knew I needed to proceed with caution.

Naturally, upon entering a warehouse club for the first time, I was dazzled by the taste tests (beef jerky! cherries! coffee! protein bars!), the Jones New York T-shirts for ten bucks, and mostly, the stunning array of recent books I've been lusting after, discounted by ten bucks or more a pop from what my local bookstore was charging. As a small bookseller's daughter, though, there's no way I was going to take business away from my local indie bookstore. But that's just my little soapbox.

I did almost cave in and buy the $40 membership for what appeared to be a staggering deal on pine nuts. Ah, but I love the humble pignoli! Yet, I restrained myself, and was later glad I did.

Nope, this newly thrifty chick had a list, and she was sticking to it. Here's how my comparison shopping trip shook out:

1. Fruit juice snacks: Wholesale Club: $6.49 for 24 bags of fruit snacks =$0.27 per bag. I thought this was a good deal, but suspected I could do better. I could. My grocery store: $2 for 10 bags = $0.20 a bag. Plus, these

※ ※ ※

snacks are shaped like letters of the alphabet, and there are little phonics cards you can cut out from the box to spell words with your child. There's nothing like them for teaching a little one to read!

2. Brand-name rice: Wholesale Club: $5.30 for 72 ounces of rice = $0.073 per ounce. My grocery store: $2.69 for 14 ounces = $0.192 per ounce. (Obviously, something like rice, which a family goes through like water, is a stellar bulk buy. And I love the idea of not running out of rice all the time.)

3. Brand-name coffee: Wholesale Club: $17.82 for 420 cups = $0.042 per cup. My grocery store: $7.49 for 270 cups (this is what the canister promises) = $0.022 per cup.

4. Name-brand olive oil: Wholesale club: $0.20 per ounce. My grocery store: $0.47 per ounce for the same brand in a much smaller bottle.

5. Name-brand cereal: $6.26 for 49 ounces = $0.12 per ounce. My grocery store: $4.79 for 18 ounces = $0.23 per ounce.

Obviously, not everything bought in bulk is a bargain. But since we go through a ton of rice, and my twelve-year-old son eats more cereal than Jerry Seinfeld, those two items would definitely be worth buying in volume. The pine nuts were a steal too. (Wholesale club: $14.28 for 15 ounces = $0.95 an ounce. My grocery store: $6.99 for 5 ounces = $1.39 per

※ ※ ※

ounce). But once I did the math, I was glad I didn't fork over $40 for a membership to save $6.60.

> Curious about bulk shopping, I embarked on an exploratory field trip to compare prices between the local warehouse club store and my local grocery store.

I know bulk aficionados would say that I would potentially save far, far more than $6.60 over multiple trips and multiple savings. But I still have my doubts. We live about twenty-five minutes from the nearest warehouse club, and that has to be taken into consideration too. Would we drive that far to save $20 to $30 on groceries every other week? Clearly, millions of people do, but for us it's hard enough to get to the grocery store as it is.

If you do love the largesse, though, I've gathered up some tips for savvy bulk buying:

- **Bring a list and do not depart from it**, because at a Sam's Club or a Costco, the stakes are even higher if you don't have a list: you could end up being stuck with a crate of something that is nothing more than an impulse purchase.
- **Use discretion**, because wasted food is expensive food. Unlike the Amish, we generally don't have the

⁂ ⁂ ⁂

knack for utilizing every scrap of food we buy, and masses go to waste. "We waste enough food to fill the Rose Bowl every day," said Jonathan Bloom of the Web site wastedfood.com. In fact, "40% of the food produced for consumption in the U.S. never will be eaten" (Sharon Palmer, "Paying the high price of food waste," *SunSentinel*, May 11, 2010). In a world of hunger and need, this is definitely a sickening statistic. Still, it's so easy to amass food items bought at the clubs, and then end up like Jason: "We've bought bulk packages of cheddar cheese, Popsicles, honey that crystallized way before we were done using the entire jar, and oranges and other fruits, only to end up throwing away much of it because it expired before we could use it all."

Friends Don't Let Friends Rationalize Dumb Bulk Buys

It's just not logical to buy a 50-gallon drum of shampoo, so don't justify it because the price per ounce has stupefied you beyond all reason. This completely defeats the purpose of buying in bulk, which is saving money on things you need to buy.

Ask yourself, "Am I rationalizing this buy?" and if it has to be justified, it's probably not justifiable. Or bring a straight-shooting pal who will, if needed, drag you away from that vat of barbecue sauce. You'll thank her later.

✕ ✕ ✕

- **Consider storage**. Don't go hog wild, bulk crazy unless you use what you buy and have room to store it. Some folks have reportedly moved to another place so they have a spare room to store all their bargains! Sounds like a problem to me, not that I don't have a few spending issues of my own. Others buy an extra freezer to hold all those bags of tortellini and mini corn dogs—yikes!

Don't Buy in Bulk . . .

Seth Fiegerman of the money blog Mainstreet has some dos and don'ts for volume shopping in his article "Best Stuff NOT to Buy in Bulk" (March 29, 2010). A few of his don'ts:

1. Brown rice: "In general, we tend to think of rice as something that just lasts and lasts, but brown rice (which happens to be better for you than white rice) has a much shorter shelf life because it contains more oil."
2. Candy: "One key rule of buying in bulk is that you should beware of purchasing guilty pleasures like candy and other junk food. Otherwise, bulk buying can turn into bulk eating."

    One consumer, he said, nailed it on SavingAdvice. com: "If I go to my local store and [buy] 2 candy bars for $1 a piece," she reported, "I spend $2 and they will

※ ※ ※

last a week. I buy a box at Costco of 24 candy bars for $12, they still will be gone in a week. Even though the unit price is less, I end up spending more."

3. Paper towels and toilet paper: If storage is an issue, skip the mass paper products, said Fiegerman. "Bulk items that are light on your wallet can weigh down your life in other ways."

4. Nuts: Because nuts usually expire within two months, unless you munch on them all day long, avoid buying them in great quantities.

> Bulk items that are light on your wallet can weigh down your life in other ways.

5. Liquid hand soap: "An item that I don't think I will ever buy in bulk again is soap," says a poster on momlogic.com. "We had a thing of hand soap for almost 2 years and in about the last 6 months it turned into clotted jelly."

Do Buy in Bulk . . .

1. Cereal: If you love your brand of cereal (Cheerios!), you likely won't get sick of it, and you can save up to 40 percent by buying a really, really big box (there are usually two bags in the big boxes, so the toasty little o's won't go stale on you).

2. Soup: Canned soup keeps, and stocking up can be

⌘ ⌘ ⌘

comforting to your wallet as well as your soul on a cold, sniffly day.

3. Dog and cat food: There's nothing worse than running out of pet food. We have a very mournful-looking basset hound named Dinah who looks even more mournful when we run out of her food. This usually prompts me to microwave a chicken breast for her or open a can of tuna, which is absurd, but makes her deliriously happy and makes me feel less guilty. I've done the same for the cats. How much better to have a mondo bag of dog food and cat food on hand so it doesn't come down to that?

4. Diapers: Well, there is one thing worse than running out of pet food: running out of diapers! Those years are, thankfully, behind us; however, I do recall spending $70 or more per month on diapers. Had I shopped at Costco during the diaper years, I could have saved $17.50 per month, or 25 percent.

5. Tuna: Canned tuna also keeps, and if you buy in bulk, you can save up to 47 percent. And there's nothing fishy about that deal.

The Verdict

Though I don't think extensive quantity shopping is for me, I did pick up a principle that, prior to this Amish money probe, had failed to penetrate my thick skull. From now on, I'm going to be looking at the *unit price*, that tiny little number on

✖ ✖ ✖

stores' price stickers. This is the magic number that revealed, for one, that I was getting a better deal on a 10-packet box of fruit juice snacks from my grocery store than the bulk box of 24 packets from the warehouse club. (Just because it's in a big box, it doesn't necessarily mean it's cheaper.)

And I'm going to start watching more closely for sales and stocking up on things I know we will use up, such as toilet paper, paper towels, canned soups, and tuna. Doyle hates to run out of paper products in the worst way, and would fill the garage with a pyramid of paper if it meant never running out. I was always more of the mind-set that running out of stuff was just life, but after examining bulk buying, I realize one can be more proactive and less reactive when it comes to these things. Yes, dear, you were right!

While it makes total sense for Ella to buy gallons of apple butter and pounds of dried apples at a time, she has established herself as a heavyweight baker. Actually, all Amish women have established themselves as heavyweight bakers, while I am more of a pinweight in the baking department. Ella is Muhammad Ali, and I am the 90-pound kid from the middle school who barely made the boxing team.

Those Amish baking giants can definitely take advantage of volume discounts offered at bulk stores, and they are such genius planners that they won't waste the food.

Certainly, not a single dried apple ring went to waste that afternoon in Ella's kitchen. As I rose from my seat at her kitchen table, I counted fifteen pie shells, and she had started to pour the filling into each. When I entered her home, forty-five minutes earlier, the table was clear and the only evidences of baking were those gallon tins of apple butter.

Astounded anew, I thanked the sweet lady and stumbled out to my car. They may be unplugged, informally educated, and doggedly committed to 1693, but as long as the Amish keep having fourteen children and making fifteen pies in forty-five minutes, they will undoubtedly flourish.

MY AMISH MONEY MAKEOVER

Keen planners, the Amish are not slaves to convenience, like we are. They opt instead to plan way ahead and stock up on just about everything they need. They are bananas for bulk, and almost always buy in quantity.

TO DO: Have you tried bulk shopping at a club warehouse before? If not, make a list of five things you need, as I did, and compare their prices at your regular grocery store to the warehouse prices. Too time-consuming? Just remember to always check out the unit price, the tiny little number that should be on a shelf sticker right below the item. That figure is more indicative of value than the item price, and you'll quickly see how that's the number that will help you save bucks.

_____

_____

_____

_____

_____

✖ ✖ ✖

12

AMISH FOODIES OR
FRUGAL *FEINSCHMECKERS*

I never knew kale was so beautiful.

Actually, I never knew kale, period, before Atlee filled my bushel basket up with the firstfruits of his garden's summer abundance. (I thought it was sort of like an artichoke. As it turns out, not at all.)

In the basket, besides the pine-tree green, glossy kale, were bright bunches of crunchy lettuce; pink stalks of rhubarb; two pints of gleaming, ruby red Michigan strawberries at their peak; and one neon yellow summer squash.

The farmer's daughters greeted me at the farmhouse door,

✗ ✗ ✗

smiling as always. Sarah told me her dad was in the barn, but her mom was in the bedroom, "with the baby." She dimpled with pleasure at sharing this special news.

Fewer than forty-eight hours before, Atlee had become a father for the eighth time; baby John could now be heard exercising his lungs. Atlee led us out to the garden, where he filled our bushel basket and chatted about what was growing.

"At the beginning of the [growing season], the basket might seem kind of empty," he said apologetically. "By the end of the summer, though, we won't be able to fit it all in there."

Meanwhile, I was thinking, *I've never owned so many vegetables in my life! What in the world am I going to do with it all?*

Atlee and I wandered around the farm, petting a highly pregnant sheep, avoiding chickens and ducks, and inhaling the sweet smell of clover in the fields. It was our first vegetable share pick-up, and we couldn't have asked for a more idyllic day.

I asked Atlee if he was also selling his cheese today. "*Ja,*" he said. "It's an aged, raw milk cheese. You could compare it to Gouda or baby Swiss."

Raw milk cheese, I later discovered, has more vitamins and minerals in it than pasteurized milk cheese. Atlee crafts and ages the cheese right on the farm, using the fresh milk of grass-fed cows.

To be honest, he had me at "fresh cheese," and it was a done deal even before he told me he charged $5 a pound.

⋇ ⋇ ⋇

Five bucks? For a pound of farm-crafted, aged, hand-cut, raw milk, organic cheese? I don't know if Atlee had heard the word *artisanal*, but this creamy, pungent wedge no doubt qualifies.

I've always daydreamed of quitting my day job and becoming a fromagier—perhaps Atlee's cheese is the first step on my journey.

At any rate, I paid a paltry price for some sumptuous cheese (a pound of regular, nonorganic Gouda at my grocer is $12, imported from the Netherlands). The vegetables and fruits were priced well, too, at about $1.15 a pound (a pint alone of organic California strawberries at the grocery store is $4). Even when we threw in $5 for gas and $20 for the CSA (Community Supported Agriculture) membership, the produce was still a fair deal.

When we got home, I Googled *kale* and found out that it's like spinach or mustard greens, and that Bobby Flay has a killer recipe for the brilliantly green leaves, sautéed in garlic and olive oil, broth, and red wine vinegar. We also sautéed the summer squash, tossed the veggies in pasta, and whipped up some strawberry shortcake.

That night we ate like kings and queens. That glorious yet simple meal of veggies (starring the demystified kale), pasta, strawberries and cake—as the Amish say—"eats real good."

"Kids," I said, sensing a teachable moment, "this food was just in the *ground* a couple of hours ago!"

They nodded as they chewed, obviously not as impressed

⌘ ⌘ ⌘

as Mom, but hopefully the message was sinking in with my city offspring: food doesn't arrive on this earth encased in bubble wrap at the grocery store.

There's no dollar value I can place on that lesson, but much to my frugal foodie delight, you can save money by buying food directly from the farmer (more on that later). It's the next best thing to what most Amish folks do, which is grow, butcher, cure, pickle, and bake their own food.

"The Amish are creative with what they eat, and they eat a lot of what they produce themselves—which is the cheapest way to feed yourself," said Erik Wesner. "Nearly all Amish homes have a sizable garden, which the mother and children tend. When I'm staying with Amish friends on the farm—which is part-dairy, part-produce—we eat some variety of eggs, milk, maybe a simple pie, cheese, and lots of fresh produce, like tomatoes—boy, the tomatoes!—and lettuce and other fresh, good stuff in the summer."

> A glorious yet simple meal of veggies (starring the demystified kale), pasta, strawberries and cake—as the Amish say—"eats real good."

Bishop Eli was practically smacking his lips when I asked him about frugal food sourcing.

"The best, most economical meal, in my opinion," he said, eyes lit up like an LED flashlight, "is potatoes, beans, and corn we grow in our gardens, and meat we butcher ourselves."

The Amish may know the value of a dollar, but make no mistake: they are major connoisseurs of food from soup to nuts. In fact, their passion for food is such that they refer to themselves as *feinschmeckers*, which translates to "people who eat well and plenty," or "Amish foodies."

A couple of their favorite mottos underscore their zest for yum on the cheap:

1. "No woman can be happy with less than seven to cook for."
2. "A plump wife and a big barn never did any man harm."

Hmmm. Let's hope it doesn't come to that, the "plump wife" part anyway. Just writing this chapter is making me hungry.

GRAPE MUSH AND OTHER *Gut* FOODS

Ever wondered what those frugal *feinschmeckers* eat, besides brown butter noodles and shoofly pie? By the way, they do eat shoofly pie, which, in keeping with Amish thrift, costs little to make.

"Shoofly pie is a very cheap pie!" Banker Bill exclaimed upon my mentioning the famous Amish dessert. "There's— what?—four ingredients?" Actually, Bill, there are six elements that go into shoofly pie: flour, brown sugar, lard or shortening, molasses, eggs, and soda, seven ingredients if you count

※ ※ ※

the pie shell, but still, it's a parsimonious dessert if there ever was one.

You would think, upon visiting Lancaster County, that the Plain folk top off each and every meal with a slice of their illustrious pie, so named because cooks would traditionally cool it on a windowsill, where its supersweet aroma would attract flies. But it's actually a once-in-a-while dessert for the People, who, with gardens and orchards and fresh milk and eggs in abundance, have a wide repertoire of desserts under their bonnets.

Following are three actual meal menus from an Amish family. Each meal includes homemade bread, farm-churned butter, and home-canned jelly:

- Breakfast: Eggs, cornmeal mush with ketchup, oatmeal with raisins, applesauce. "There's nothing cheaper for breakfast than cornmeal mush and eggs," Ella Yoder said.
- Dinner (lunch): Beef and carrots, scalloped potatoes, gravy, baked corn, carrot salad, graham cracker pudding, cookies, peaches.
- Supper: Vegetable soup, bologna, tomatoes and Chinese cabbage, apple sauce, chowchow, apple dumplings with milk and sugar.

Was anyone else surprised by bologna making it onto an Amish menu? It seems very 1970s, not 1770s, and also

※ ※ ※

highly processed. To my relief, I discovered the Amish do not buy shrink-wrapped packets of bologna, but rather process it themselves with their own, more natural curing techniques.

Plain cooks actually make a lot of simple, filling recipes that are go-to entrées in any modern family's kitchen, such as Sloppy Joes (or *Does*, if venison is used), spaghetti, and pizza. Naturally, they don't grab a can of Manwich from the pantry; they use their own home-canned sauces. "Pizza is a treat, but I like my own better," said Abigail. "I use homemade dough and can my own pizza sauce, plus I use fresh cheese from our cows' milk here."

Suddenly, I have a hankering for homemade pizza—how about you?

Amish cooks also have their specialties, such as shoofly pie, chowchow, and snitz pie, not to mention grape mush, which I had never heard of before Fern mentioned it as a thrifty dessert or sweet side dish. This purple pottage, a cus-tard/pudding-type thing, calls for homemade grape juice, sugar, Jell-O, lemons, and tapioca. Some folks slather it on pancakes, but Banker Bill found another use for it: "I had it on pumpkin pie," he said. "It was surprisingly good."

Speaking of Banker Bill, he told me that the Amish love to eat, but they always stick to cheap ingredients accessible in their gardens, root cellars, or barns (cows' milk, cheese, etc.). "If you go to an Amishman's home for a meal, you're not getting shrimp—that's just not going to happen," he said.

❈ ❈ ❈

"They eat hearty, starchy foods, which are incredibly cheap, like potatoes, and they burn it all off that afternoon."

CHOWCHOW, ANYONE?

Let's talk chowchow for a minute. You may have skipped the introduction, which mentions that chowchow is one culinary link between the Amish and the Mennonites and their shared history. I actually grew up with chowchow, as a mainstay of "*faspa*," a light supper, served early on Sundays, consisting of buns; cold cuts; pickled salads (such as chowchow) and sweet, creamy cucumber salad; cheese; and cookies—a no-cook meal designed so women did not have to work on the day of rest.

Chowchow is comprised of vegetables, like carrots, peppers, and cauliflower, with kidney beans, navy beans, and lima beans, pickled in a brine of vinegar, sugar, turmeric, and celery seed. This dish adds a nice sassy zing to the starchier aspects of the Amish/Mennonite palate, along with other pickles, relishes, and condiments for which Plain cooks are rightfully famous. Oddly enough, when I was in Korea a few years ago to pick up our Korean daughter, the many little dishes of pickled radishes and kimchi at every meal reminded me of the vitality and dynamism of chowchow.

✖ ✖ ✖

At a large noontime Amish meal, chowchow will be served as part of their traditional "seven sweets and seven sours," the supporting cast for mounds of protein and starch. Among the essentials of seven sweets and seven sours are pepper cabbage, red beet pickled eggs, five-cup salad with marshmallows and pineapples, coleslaw, and brown sugar pears.

Farm to Table: Shake the Hand That Feeds You

Most of us Fancies don't have chickens pecking away on our lawns, yard eggs to collect, or even large gardens from which to harvest delicious bunches of kale and strawberries. And there sure aren't any cows in my garage, awaiting their final destinies as burgers, steaks, and roasts. How could I possibly apply this particular Amish money secret—producing one's own food—and make it work for my family, living in the middle of Grand Rapids?

I was amazed and gratified to find out that I could buy food directly from a farmer and save a bundle. Not only could I save money on groceries, but also my family could routinely visit a farm where the cows are happy and the beef is extra-delicious—and nourishing. Beef and milk from grass-fed livestock and eggs from land-grazing chickens better their mass-produced counterparts in Omega-3 fatty acids, not to mention vitamins A and E. The meat is also substantially less

※ ※ ※

fatty than that of confined cows who lunch on soybeans and corn instead of grass.

Atlee's contented cows produce a delectable meat that is tender and permeated with good fat and deep, flavorful beefiness. I had read that humanely raised meat can cost up to twice as much as the industrially produced stuff, so I was shocked when I found out that's just not the case when you buy directly from the farmer.

Because we don't yet have a deep freezer, and we have to store our frozen meat on one side of our fridge, we couldn't buy an entire cow. We ended up "cow pooling," splitting a quarter of a side of beef with Doyle's parents; both of us ended up with about 72 pounds each. Atlee suggested we get a third each of ground beef, roasts, and steaks—that's what his other cow poolers often do—and that's what we did. Some beef buyers team up with up to five other families to buy a side of beef from Atlee. "They negotiate who gets what cuts," he said.

> How could I possibly apply this particular Amish money secret—producing one's own food—and make it work for my family, living in the middle of Grand Rapids?

Are you sitting down? Forgive me for being a little dramatic, but the deal we got on Atlee's beef was nothing short of a meaty marvel: $2.10 a pound! You can't even get a regular, frozen brick of hamburger from the grocery store for that, never mind grass-fed, natural, organic T-bone and porterhouse steaks. We had rarely ever bought steaks because they were too expensive. Now we had 23 pounds of it in our freezer.

I had a hard time comparing prices on the meat, because my grocer didn't carry a lot of grass-fed, natural beef. So I had to go online, and what I found astonished me and made me a local farmer cow-pooler for life.

	Atlee's beef, per pound	Online grass fed, natural beef, per pound (without shipping)
Sirloin steak	$2.10	$14.00
Flank steak	$2.10	$12.25
Ground beef	$2.10	$8.00
Ribeye steak	$2.10	$18.00
Porterhouse	$2.10	$19.00

On the ground beef alone (we received about 23 pounds of it), we saved $135, and far more on the roasts and steaks.

"But," you might say, "we weren't planning on buying organic, grass-fed beef anyway, so we wouldn't save that much money." You're right, smarty-pants; you wouldn't save a mountain of money if you compare Atlee's meat to your basic bubble-wrapped meat at the grocery store. Let's take health, well-being, and the wonderful fringe benefit of supporting

✖ ✖ ✖

your local farmer (as opposed to some slaughterhouse con-
glomerate in another state, or even Uruguay, from which some
meat is imported) off the table, so to speak. There's still taste,
which is something to consider. Too frugal to care if your taste
buds begin to sing "I Had a Dream" after a juicy bite of grass-
fed steak? Then I commend your prudence, and ask you to
consider this: you'll still save a bunch of cash if you buy direct
from the farmer. I challenge you to find an edible ribeye for
under $7 a pound. 'Nuff said.

However, if your interest, wallet, and taste buds are piqued
by my discovery, check out your local CSA (Community
Supported Agriculture) group, which goes together on a sub-
scription with a farmer, takes turns delivering the meat and
produce, and generally makes it pretty painless to buy from a
farm-to-table guy like Atlee. He (or she) doesn't even have to be
Amish. He just has to have a green thumb and happy animals.

Mind you, don't expect to fly into your corner store and
emerge with grass-fed, organic beef for $2 to $5 a pound.
This farm-to-table business is a slower, kinder, gentler type
of food consumption. With Atlee, I wrote him a letter stating
our intentions of buying a quarter of beef. It was very quaint
and old-fashioned, although later I learned the man does have
order forms!

When our meat was ready, he called me on a shanty phone
and we arranged for a pickup time. A fifty-minute drive into
the Michigan countryside later, we were the proud owners of
a box of beef with benefits.

※ ※ ※

Michael Pollan, author of the *New York Times* best seller *In Defense of Food*, hails the power of a shortened food chain through farm-to-table: "In a short food chain, eaters can make their needs and desires known to the farmer, and farmers can impress upon eaters the distinctions between ordinary and exceptional food . . . Food reclaims its story, and some of its nobility, when the person who grew it hands it you" (New York: Penguin, 2008, 160).

We've just ordered half a pig from Atlee, for which we'll pay $1.50 a pound. I will definitely be making my semi-famous pork chops with cherry pie filling in the Crock-Pot, but maybe this year I'll buy the pie filling at the farmers market.

The Farmers Market

Less than 10 percent of the food consumed in Grand Rapids is raised locally, said Tom Carey, who runs a CSA farm nearby. That's a crying shame, but hopefully that will change as people learn about and seek locally sourced food.

No surprise at all, Lancaster County, Pennsylvania, is at or near the top of the nation in the value of farm products sold directly to consumers at CSAs, road stands, and farmers' markets. Leola Produce Market is just one Amish hot spot where you can pick up collards, chard, beets, carrots, mustard greens, and broccoli in early summer; Indian corn and pumpkins in the fall; and just about anything else under the sun in between.

※ ※ ※

These days, everyone lives near a farmers market (check out localharvest.org for one near you). To get the most economy out of buying food there, check out these tips:

- Let them eat kale (in June). If you know a bit of what to expect when you get to the farmers market, making decisions at each stall is much easier. Learn what grows when in your area, and talk to the growers about what will be coming to market in upcoming weeks.
- The early bird gets the worm . . . or does she? (Part 2) In the morning, the market boasts its best selection, and the premium produce usually goes first, and may even be sold out by the time Ms. Sleep-in-on-Saturday ambles in. But when she does wander in, she'll be the one to tote home a bag of screaming deals. Farmers usually prefer to offload their wares at a discount instead of loading them back up and lugging them home.
- Be adventurous. Your veggie rock stars, like carrots, potatoes, and onions, may be a little costlier at the market than at conventional grocery stores, because of supply and demand. However, I know that you—the thrifty, frisky you—will try ethnic, heirloom, or rare vegetables, knowing that a recipe

> Your palate will expand as your wallet contracts.

✄ ✄ ✄

is only a Google away (those of you with fancy phones can look up a recipe for chard right there at the stall!). Your palate will expand as your wallet contracts.

- Plot your meals ahead of time. Just like grocery shopping, sketching out what meals you are going to make for the next week helps you make the most of every veggie, slice of cheese, and morsel of meat you buy at the market. It also helps make the most of every penny spent. But if you do buy something off the list—and you will—and if you're just not sure what to do with those baby beets, for example, ask the farmer how he likes to eat it himself. Sometimes farmers even have recipes.

- Bring big bags and small change. Durable canvas bags, backpacks, or even baby strollers help you tote all of that inexpensive abundance with aplomb. Don't forget a couple of dollars broken up into change to make your transactions go faster and smoother. And then it's on to radishes.

Finally, let me invoke the fearsome Bishop Eli, who yanked open his shirt in the first chapter and nearly gave me a heart attack. On the topic of buying from your local farmer or just buying local in general, he is unequivocal: "We stand together, or we fall together!" he said, stabbing that gnarly finger in the air once more. On this matter, I'm with Bishop Eli. Let's stand together instead.

⌘ ⌘ ⌘

Cheaper Than You-Know-What

I don't believe any ambulatory Amish person would be caught dead without a garden. A garden is as much a given as a straw hat for men and a bonnet for ladies. Why? Why do you think? Because growing your own food is cheaper than you-know-what. From a $2.99 packet of cherry tomato seeds springs forth hundreds of juicy little orbs, and a $2.99 packet of zucchini yields what seems like a thousand of the quintessential summer veggie, so many it's impossible to use up yourself, and thus they must be left like small green babies in baskets on people's doorsteps. Gardening is mind-bogglingly frugal, which is why the Amish love it so much; that, and homegrown food is the epitome of wholesomeness.

I defer to Bishop Eli again: "Food shipped in from other countries is not fresh and has lots of preservatives. Tree-ripened fruit and garden vegetables are much better for you."

I've said before the Amish are inadvertently green, but the truth is they care a lot about keeping their food source natural. "I don't like to put chemicals in my garden," said Sadie, who runs an organic farm with her husband. "It's a lot cheaper

⌗ ⌗ ⌗

to buy seeds than it is to buy vegetables, and it's really fun to work in the garden, in the sunshine."

True confession time: I don't garden, per se, although I am growing some veggies in large containers this year.

I already admitted my phobia of worms, which makes me a big wuss, I know. But since we moved last summer, I actually have a legitimate reason for not planting a garden. Our new yard is too shady to grow anything, although we may try a grapevine over our picket fence and see how that goes.

I know nothing could be more low-cost than keeping a garden, but the bottom line is that gardening takes lots of work and time, and time costs something.

Apple Chutney to Zucchini Relish

Speaking of thrifty-yet-time-intensive activities, canning is making a comeback with us Fancies. What better way to keep some of that low-cost summer and fall bounty than to put it up and enjoy it again in the winter? According to Jarden Home Brands, maker of Kerr and Ball brands of Mason jars, sales of canning equipment were up 30 percent in 2009. It's even hip these days. There are countrywide canning fests, with chefs like NOLA's John Besh and Seattle's Heather Earnhardt contributing recipes like Sugar Plums in Syrup and Tomato Apricot Jam (Joanna Prisco, "Five Unexpected Food Trends," *Parade*, November 15, 2009).

Way ahead of the trend as usual, the Amish are exuberant

⚒ ⚒ ⚒

and veteran canners. Not only do they grow their own tomatoes and herbs, but they'll put up homemade salsa, spaghetti sauce, Sloppy Joe sauce, tomato soup, tomato juice, tomato pepper relish, and just plain old canned tomatoes.

Sigh. I love canned tomatoes, at least the ones my Grandma Loewen used to make. Maybe this year I'll can some myself, in her honor, and also in honor of Amish thrift.

"I do a lot of canning," Sadie told me. "A cheap meal in the winter is canned goods and fried potatoes."

From apple chutney to zucchini relish, the Amish know their way around a canning kettle, which, on top of growing their own produce, makes for a lot of scrumptious dining at bargain basement prices.

Schmecks Appeal

Investigating how Amish food lovers eat deliciously on a dime changed my whole outlook on food, grocery shopping, and the real value of nourishing, tasty food. And though I can't grow or produce much of my own food, I did discover how easy it is and how worthwhile to team up with a local farmer and shake the hand that feeds me. And this bears repeating: grass-fed porterhouse steak: $2.10 per pound.

That's just a crazy, silly, wacky price that happens to be true. I have heard that prices vary by state and farmer, and that people pay up to $5 or $6 per pound for CSA beef in some areas. But those are still wacky-low prices.

I'm also addicted to the farmers market. Not only are the prices great and the food fresh, but the camaraderie and community feeling gives the experience so much more worth and meaning than a mere supermarket trip.

The Amish may be extremely careful with a dollar, but they are not going to scrimp on the importance of real food well grown. Naturally, they find a way to eat like royalty for a peasant's pittance.

Frugal? Check.

Feinschmecker? Check, check.

I leave you with a maxim from the People, with loads of *schmecks* appeal: "Kissin' wears out; cookin' don't."

Now, there's some food for thought.

※ ※ ※

MY AMISH MONEY MAKEOVER

Much to my frugal foodie delight, you can save money by buying food directly from the farmer. It's the next best thing to what most Amish folks do, which is grow, butcher, cure, pickle, and bake their own food.

To Do: Google a local CSA or farm-to-table operation near you, and inquire about prices. Make room in your freezer for all the abundance, and prepare to eat like kings and queens on a peasant's pittance. Also, consider planting a garden or joining a community garden. Preserving your harvest will save you even more!

⁕ ⁕ ⁕

13

BARTERING: I'LL TRADE YOU THIS COW FOR A BUNCH OF RUGS

When Martha and Abel have enough unwearable clothes gathered, they tear them into strips and weave them into charming, color-drenched rugs. "We help each other make the rugs," said Abel. "My uncle sells them at his farm stand, but sometimes we trade them for something else. One time, we traded fifty or sixty rugs for a heifer."

⚒ ⚒ ⚒

No money changed hands in that transaction, but the trade was very much in keeping with the Amish way of wealth. For Abel and Martha and their trading partner, bartering hand-woven rugs for a heifer was a way to say, "I've got these goods; you've got this good. We both have this need; how can we shake hands?"

When things are tough, you do what you can to get what you need. In this recession, bartering has become vogue again after seventy-plus years, "a social behavior left over from the 1880s to the Great Depression," said Dr. Kraybill.

The Amish love to swap goods for goods, or goods for services, or services for services. "Within our system, if we can barter, we do," said Bishop Jake. "If we need some trucking done, we exchange it for garden products, or shop work [the farmer makes wooden furniture of all kinds on the side]. I think we do save money through bartering. We try and make a deal where each one is happy."

Fairness is key for the Amish, but if they do err, it's on the side of their trading partner. "If anything, we want to make sure [the person we're bartering with] gets a good deal."

The Amish have a long history of living outside a cash economy. With a strong community and relationships, there has always been and still is deep trust between neighbors. Farmer Abraham routinely shares his time and muscle with farmer Gideon, and with no discussion whatsoever, Gideon will invest his own sweat equity when Abraham needs help.

※ ※ ※

When Naomi's children were younger, they would have a single aunt, Aunt Katie, babysit for them. In exchange, Naomi would give her baked goods or mow her lawn for her. "We never paid her money, but we traded what we have to offer," she said.

Andy the Amish boat cover maker switches out goods and services all the time. "I can't move the boats around in the winter with a handcart," he said. "So I'll trade boat covers for a guy who has a truck and can help me move the boats."

Twice, Andy's been taken out on the Great Lakes for a charter fishing trip; he gave the charter captain a boat cover for the excursions.

"I put a top on a pontoon for this one guy, and that would have cost him $250, if he paid me," said Andy. "But in return, he has given my family the right to go fishing on his lake with his pontoon boat anytime we want. And we go down there quite a bit."

Sometimes a buggy just won't cut it. More often than not, when it's Amish exchanging with *Englishers*, the Plain folk need some kind of transportation or trucking. Freeman negotiated with his neighbor the use of his loader tractor. In exchange: "I had my boys go over and help him out at their farm for a day or two."

The more I thought about the notion of bartering, the more it made sense, especially in a money crunch like this one, when disposable income is scarce. Folks want to hold on to their cash these days, and would rather trade a day of

⌗ ⌗ ⌗

landscaping, for, say, a stay at a bed-and-breakfast, than fork over $150.

The only problem is, I'm no good at landscaping, and that is a gross understatement. The question is, what am I good at, and what could I trade for something of equal value? What are *you* good at, and what could you negotiate for something of worth?

> What are *you* good at, and what could you negotiate for something of worth?

I've had a little experience with bartering, but not much. Last year, a friend of mine, my Pilates instructor, needed to borrow our car with a trailer hitch so she could haul her daughter's new playhouse home from where it was crafted an hour away. She used our second car, which we weren't using anyway that day, for a few hours, and in return she gave me a free hour-long torture, er, Pilates lesson on her stretching rack, er, Reformer machine. Usually, she charges forty dollars for the privilege of kicking my bum. Even though every muscle hurt the next day, I still got a good deal on that trade.

We had something she could use, and in return she offered me something I needed—bum kicking.

Ann exchanged her eagle-eyed editing services with a lawyer who drew up a will for her and her husband. "Basically, it was trading our expertise and time, but it's a fair transaction, and I think we were both pleased."

✼ ✼ ✼

Listen to these Fancies and how they haggled their stuff and their skills:

- Catherine: "I like to 'rent out' my husband's computer expertise in exchange for free meals!"
- Sasha: "My husband is a chiropractor, and that has come in handy from time to time. We trade chiropractic care for haircuts with our neighbor, and have also used it to barter dental work."
- Laura: "I think bartering's a great idea in this downturn. We're currently bartering services (helping a single friend do some house projects—painting, cleaning out the garage, yard work, etc.) in exchange for a gorgeous antique 1880s Victorian oak hutch for our dining room—that we couldn't have afforded otherwise. A win-win for both of us!"
- Shelley: "My stepfather is a chiropractor, and he does this often. One example is a guy built his deck and received chiropractic treatments; another gave a granite countertop for treatments."
- Tara: "A friend of ours is a photographer, and he did pictures for us; in turn my husband, who's an attorney, did their wills. I thought it was a win-win all the way around!"
- Rachel: "I bartered a box of free books [she's an author] for some head shots. My sister-in-law is a professional photographer and she spent two

※ ※ ※

days taking pictures of me for my Web site, book promotion, etc. So in exchange I sent her a box of signed books to give to friends."

- Ellen: "In the hubster's conservative Mennonite tradition, we barter with hard work. We'll help you build your house, and then you show up at our house when we're finishing our basement. I saw it in action these last few months. Mennonites are very concerned with making sure everything is fairly traded so no one feels taken advantage of."
- Christine: "Our neighborhood is big on 'exchanging.' We exchange perennials, landscaping bricks/rocks, child care, and homemade jams. It's just one big ol' fashioned horse-trading 'club.'"

Win-Win

Notice how "win-win" comes up a few times with bartering? Barterers are often gleeful when it comes to their no-money trades. Laura, who swapped some painting, cleaning, and yard work for an antique oak hutch, hit it on the nail: "We couldn't have afforded [the 'gorgeous' piece of furniture] otherwise."

Whereas in the Depression, people struck deals in tools, chickens, and milk—essential provisions and supplies—now traders will offer personal training sessions for scuba gear or a Pilates lesson for a borrowed trailer hitch. In our recession, people probably don't have a lot of throwaway cash floating around, and even if they do, they may be a touch paranoid to part with it for something other than necessities.

Just a glance at the bartering Web site barterquest.com reveals that people are usually not trading indispensable goods and services. I checked out "Writer services," because that's my only real knack, and saw that many of the things being offered by or to my fellow writers were not strictly compulsory. Writers and editors were offering their services and wanting in return such things as music lessons, massages, Web design, and dental implants (the most necessary trade I spotted). On the flip side, those wanting to trade with a writer included a hypnotist, a life coach, an artisanal jewelry designer, and a publicist (who was obviously desperate for a scribe, or at least one who could spell; she posted a need for a "writier").

> In our recession, people probably don't have a lot of throwaway cash floating around.

The jewelry designer snagged my attention. Will Work for Jewelry? I thought I would give it a whirl, especially when I saw the links to her vivid, one-of-a-kind creations. "I will need a pitch letter targeted to fahion [she also needs a little help spelling] editors- introducing my jewelry collection. I'm also considering having this same person create a press kit."

My proficiencies are limited: I can't sew, cook in quantity, teach a musical instrument, design a Web site, or give someone a massage, hypnosis, or dental implants. But I can probably compose a nifty pitch letter that'll blow the Jimmy Choos off those fashion editors.

Pork for Tuition

Bartering postings on Craigslist have increased 100 percent since last year, and even if the cable company probably won't take a couple of lasagnas for HBO and Showtime, you'd be surprised at who would.

A 2010 article in Lancaster, Pennsylvania's *Sunday News* featured a fascinating bartering opportunity that's been going on for years at a Missouri college:

> In St. Charles, Mo., Lindenwood University will consider taking meat from farmers who cannot afford to pay their children's tuition in cash. Some 20 or so students have attended the university under that deal.
>
> "It was pure barter. Pork or beef for tuition," said Lindenwood spokesman Scott Queen. "We gave them market value for their beef or pork, which was far more than they could have gotten selling it off—since the middlemen were taking much of the profit. It was Lindenwood's way of honoring the hardworking farm families and helping keep kids in school."

※ ※ ※

Queen said interest in the barter offer has tapered off in the past few years. "The door is still open, though, especially considering these difficult economic times," he added. (Suzanne Kennedy, "'Trade you my bike for dental work," *Sunday News* [Lancaster, PA], April 26, 2009).

"We Both Got Exactly What We Wanted"

It's no surprise that the Amish, whose lives are deeply interwoven with those of their community members, have kept bartering alive and well. For the Plain folk, nice trade-offs aren't a trendy way to surf the recession, but just business as usual. We who live less connected lives may find it awkward to negotiate with someone toward value for value. But in foreign countries, trading and haggling over prices are widespread practices.

"Americans can be too proud to barter," said Angela Blyker, a writer friend who has spent lots of time overseas doing missions work. Her husband, Ben, is a pastor/carpenter/handyman/jack-of-all-trades who grew up in Mexico, and who feels completely comfortable with the notion of trading services and goods.

"Bartering actually builds relationships, as people have to engage on a deeper level when they must express need. It makes you also think of your assets first, before your needs. It is surprising how many 'assets' we all have been given

❊ ❊ ❊

by God to share! Trading with your neighbors builds community, and who has done this better in the States than the Amish?"

The Amish are stellar community builders, and they've been bartering for hundreds of years. They know better than anyone that when you're taking something in trade, you have to be a pretty good judge. Because as Ella found out, there are good deals, and then there's the right deal.

Years ago, when she was delivering one of her children, Ella traded a midwife's services for a handmade appliquéd Amish quilt. "On my end, definitely it was a good deal," she said about the barter. "And on her end it worked well too. We both got exactly what we wanted from the deal."

Switch, Swap, Haggle, Higgle

Check out these bartering Web sites to get started:

Barterquest.com
JoeBarter.com
SwapThing.com
U-Exchange.com
Craigslist.org

Let's Swap

"Swap parties," said writer Alexandra Fix, "have made the old system of barter delightfully new."

✕ ✕ ✕

Last spring, she and her sewing club buddies put on an afternoon yarn swap. They each brought superfluous supplies from their hoard at home—single balls of yarn, multiple skeins, socks and scarves, knit and crochet books, old patterns, and duplicate needles.

"We arranged our goods on a kitchen island and served coffee, tea, and munchies at the nearby dining table," she wrote. "Then we casually wandered around the yarn display, ate, drank, chatted and selected treasures from each other's stash."

The pals bagged the remaining yarn and supplies and donated it to a yarn shop accepting donations for a missionary group teaching knitting to women in Mozambique ("Let's Swap by Alexandra Fix," *Women's LifeStyle*, May 2010).

Call it bartering with snacks, but the swap party has definitely arrived, bringing with it freebies in the form of clothes, prom dresses, baby wear, art materials, craft supplies, toys, and books. A swap meet is better than a garage sale, even, because you usually organize it with friends (i.e., people with similar tastes and stages of life), and everything is free. *Free!*

In an effort to conquer clutter and share as a community, my moms group put on a swap meet a couple of months ago. I had my doubts as to how much stuff I might *get*, but I liked the idea of offloading a box of clothes we had all outgrown.

Once again, I was delightfully surprised. Clothes were sorted by size and gender, from newborn onesies to men's

✄ ✄ ✄

clothing, making it so easy to pick out what we wanted and needed. I got a pair of cute black capris, a summer tank top, a book about friendship I had always wanted, and a brand-new container of Neutrogena hand cream.

But the most remarkable swap item was bellowing Doyle's name, not mine. It was a beautifully illustrated book about the fur trade, in great shape.

Now, let me back up a minute. My dear husband has fantasies about being a voyageur, wearing a beaver hat and paddling up some far-flung river in a canoe weighed down with pelts, on his way to a shore lunch of fish, pemmican, and rubaboo, a type of porridge featuring corn, bear grease, flour, and maple sugar.

He was tickled pink with the book, and for a time regaled me with voyageur lore: "Did you know the fur traders had to be able to carry two ninety-pound bundles of fur over portage, and more suffered from strangulated hernias than any other injury?"

That I did not know. However, I knew an extraordinary gift for Doyle when I saw one, an extraordinary *free* gift, which, more than any other anecdote in this tome, underscores the "one man's trash is another's treasure" slogan.

I estimate I got $65 worth of clothing, books, and lotion for *nada*! I'm now planning a book swap party for later in the summer. I'm one of those impractical people who like to own books, not borrow them from friends or the library. A book swap, I figure, will allow me to divest myself of a small pile of

⚒ ⚒ ⚒

books I'm not attached to and gain a small pile of new-to-me reading material. My pals can do the same.

Some swap party pointers:

- The ideal number of "shoppers" is 10–15 if the event is at someone's home. Our moms group has about 25, and that was fine.
- Suggest a ballpark number of items to bring to avoid a major imbalance in trade options. I'm inviting my book swap guests to bring five hardcover and/or five trade paperback books each.
- Hand out a poker chip or token for each item brought to the table. These chips can be "spent" on items once the sale begins, so that each participant takes home the same number of items she brought—so yin and yang, that.
- If you do a jewelry swap, say, have everyone pick a number and conduct the proceedings white elephant–style. The lucky duck who picks #1 gets first dibs on the loot, unless, of course, you incorporate stealing, which means several other people might steal and re-steal the first choice. We do a white elephant exchange every Christmas with Doyle's cousins, and I look forward to my fiery rivalry with his cousin's wife, Patti, more than I look forward to the item I bring home. Things can get out of hand—let's just put it that way.

※ ※ ※

Deluxe Re-gifting

Holding on to your hard-earned money and still getting some things you want and need? Now, that's slick.

Holding on to your hard-earned money and still getting some things you want and need? Now, that's slick.

Like the Amish, we Fancies can offer up what we know how to do and get paid in services other people know how to perform, or in stuff they have lying around. Rob, for example, knew his wife wouldn't be too impressed with him shelling out their limited discretionary money for golf clubs and accessories. But when he found someone wanting to barter some really nice golf clubs for his skills rewiring a chandelier, he got what he wanted for an evening's worth of work. Really, bartering is re-gifting taken to the next level.

My dream barter: a week on someone's lakefront cottage, someone who needs a book proposal written, that is. We don't have the cash lying around to pay for a cottage rental, but if there's one thing I know how to do, it's write a book proposal! Who was it who said everyone's got a book in them? At the very least, everyone seems to *think* they have a book in them. As I keep dreaming about lapping blue waves and sand between my toes, I'll also keep working the bartering Web sites and inviting trade propositions. It's definitely a plan. (Please contact me on my blog if you're interested. *-wink-*)

⚒ ⚒ ⚒

MY AMISH MONEY MAKEOVER

For centuries, the Amish have bartered with one another and *Englishers* too, trading their skills and goods for their neighbors'. Often, both parties get exactly what they want, and no money has changed hands.

TO DO: What services or skills do you have that you could trade for something else? Find a bartering Web site that suits you, and post your goods and services; also, post the goods and services you'd love to acquire in trade. Start asking around your circle of friends and acquaintances for bartering opportunities, or post what you've got to offer on a social networking site. Think about stuff lying around your house, like the Precious Moments figurine collection Great-Aunt Edna left you in her will. Throw a swap party with your pals or by yourself. You'll offload stuff you don't want and gain stuff you do want—for free!

❈ ❈ ❈

14

THE BEST THINGS IN LIFE
ARE FREE

E verybody's safe."
That's what the sign says in front of my friend Alison's charred husk of a house.

Just yesterday, Doyle and I were awakened by the phone ringing. The caller, a friend, told us some extremely disturbing news: her mother had driven by Alison and Paul's house earlier that morning and saw that it had burned down. "There's just nothing there," she said, but couldn't tell me anything else.

For fifteen minutes, I didn't know if my beloved friend and her family were alive or dead.

✕ ✕ ✕

My overriding thought was that surely not everyone could have escaped a blaze like that.

After what seemed like infinity, I reached Alison's sister. "Everyone got out, even Jack [their dog]," she said. "No one has even a scratch." Relief swamped me, yet the agony of those minutes of not knowing their fate will stay a long time.

At 5 a.m., Alison was up reading (typical), and she smelled smoke. Just a couple of weeks before, they had moved their bedroom to the space over the garage, where the fire had mysteriously started. Smoke alarms began to blare, and she and Paul jumped out of bed to evacuate their three children. Their son, Christopher, is deaf; he had to be slapped on the leg by his frantic mother before he woke up.

Little Eden, seven, grabbed a box with a baby bird in it. Just before bedtime, Eden had found the struggling wee thing in their yard and vowed to nurse it back to health.

Together, Paul, Alison, Christopher, Lydia, and Eden, plus Jack the dog and Max the baby bird, huddled in shock and awe as they watched their home swallowed up in flames. Alison looked at Paul over their children's heads. "We have everything we need right here."

VALUABLE

Andy Miller can also remember a moment in time when everything faded to black except for the well-being of his loved ones.

※ ※ ※

A few years ago, his two young sons took the family buggy out for a drive on a Saturday morning. They wanted to go fishing at an *Englisher* friend's lakefront property. A car, the driver blinded by the morning sunlight, came up over a hill and didn't see the buggy in his path until it was too late.

Andy's two sons were thrown like rag dolls from the buggy; nine-year-old Jonas had to be airlifted to Grand Rapids with critical injuries. His seven-year-old brother was bloody and bruised, but okay. Jonas pulled through, and to this day his *datt* keeps a photo of the crumpled buggy close at hand, to remind him of what's important.

"For me, the best times of my life have been spent with my family," Andy said. "Having devotions together, or, in the summertime, playing croquet or shuffleboard or Dutch Blitz are wonderful memories. After the accident, I realized my family and I . . . we have more than we need."

Ella Yoder was reflective when we talked about what's valuable in life. "I have learned through losing loved ones that it's so important to look forward to life's little pleasures," she said. "Coffee in the morn-

> The truth that transcends Plain and Fancy: chasing after money and things is meaningless, because the best things in life are free.

ing, listening to the birds, getting together as families."

She and three friends get together once a month and play

※ ※ ※

Scrabble. Her most cherished memories are of when she was raising her children. "We would have picnics and play hide-and-seek together," she said. "Nothing is more valuable than that."

Alison, Andy, and Ella now know what every eighty-five-year-old knows, the truth that transcends Plain and Fancy: chasing after money and things is meaningless, because the best things in life are free.

Amish Trivial Pursuit Night

Ella, Naomi, Ephraim, Daniel, and Banker Bill were barely aware I was there, such was the competitive fever permeating Amish Trivial Pursuit night.

Wild horses could not have dragged me from the occasion. My Amish posse had put on a night of fun, frivolity, and trivia just for me and my family. It was, as always, ladies versus men, and according to Banker Bill, the ladies had never won once. As an entertainment writer, I felt sure I could come alongside the ladies and help them to their first victory. The bad news was, the Amish throw out the arts and entertainment pie and replace it with Bible trivia. The good news: I went to Bible college for four years.

Abigail, the hostess, bustled around her kitchen, near where we all sat at a long table with benches. She refilled juice pitchers; replenished trays of treats, such as "bachelor button" candies, cheese curls, and popcorn dribbled with melted

✖ ✖ ✖

chocolate and caramel; and pushed those treats upon the newcomers.

Despite my Bible college education, I might as well have been a Rastafarian for all the good I did my team of ladies. I had no clue about the first few questions, until suddenly there was one I could answer, in the sports category.

"What do Joe DiMaggio and Arthur Miller have in common?" Daniel read from the question card.

"They were both married to Marilyn Monroe!" I blurted out.

There was a moment of silence. No one argued with me. Daniel flipped the card over and nodded, shrugging. "She's right."

> Even the priciest event planner in Hollywood couldn't have orchestrated the camaraderie, coziness, and fun of this simple Amish game night.

The ladies looked at me approvingly. Finally, their Great White and Fancy Hope had come through. All my years of reading *People* magazine had stood me in good stead for that moment.

The next question was read, and I looked around the room, seeing happy faces—it was plain to see that everyone was having a ball. About fifteen Amish folk mingled at the long table with the five visiting *Englisher* friends. Partygoers argued good-naturedly over the questions, and the ladies' ringleader,

※ ※ ※

a boisterous Amish gal named Rebecca, talked her team in and out of various answers, igniting raucous laughter at times. Even the priciest event planner in Hollywood couldn't have orchestrated the camaraderie, coziness, and fun of this simple Amish game night. I was a stranger to most of the guests, yet I felt completely comfortable, welcomed, at-home, and at peace.

My mind rewound to various parties, book club meetings, and dinner parties I've hosted over the years, events where I've spent way too much to finance swanky party gifts and up-market appetizers, wine, and flowers, not just to treat my guests but also—I must admit—to impress them.

Meanwhile, those overpriced affairs couldn't hold a candle to a no-fuss Amish party with chocolate-covered popcorn and a game—bought at a secondhand store—as its cornerstone.

Rightsizing

I never realized quite how much I bought into our culture's way of looking at spending and money management, how mindlessly I bought things and how recklessly I lived on the edge, before two things happened.

1. I began to spend time with the Amish, and unconsciously at the first, started to follow their example of saving, sharing, and living more simply.
2. The recession hit us square when we tried—and failed— to sell the house we had spent ten years investing in.

Such times call for a different mentality, one of reassessing spending habits and values, and of focusing not on what we lost but what we have.

Sociologists call this downturn rebalancing "rightsizing." Like most people, I was resistant at first to all the changes, but then I realized this was a good-for-me shift, from wanting more than I could get to valuing the things in life that yield true rewards.

Clearly, before this shift, my money habits—and therefore my life—were out of whack. I wanted things I couldn't afford, and sometimes I bought those things on credit. I was living on a tightrope, believing nothing bad would ever happen, so why experience a moment's discomfort denying myself so I could build a shelter against a rainy day?

I also deeply held the idea—though I didn't know it—that to build memories and have fun, you have to empty your wallet in the process.

Sadie was incredulous when I told her how much we spend on popcorn alone at the movies. "Six dollars? For popcorn?" (There's a 900 percent markup on movie popcorn; it's one of the most jacked-up items one could possibly buy.) She couldn't believe it, and she loves popcorn. Every Sunday night, she and her husband and their children play dominoes and share a huge bowl of fluffy popped kernels, drizzled with butter.

"We have fun without spending very much money," she said. "We play volleyball, or cook hot dogs after a hike in the woods."

※ ※ ※

My family and I are great movie buffs, so no doubt we'll continue to patronize our local Cineplex, and we may still pay the 900 percent markup on popcorn because it's like buttery, salty, melt-in-your-mouth gold, after all. Post-rightsizing, though, pricey movie nights (seventy-five bucks for movie tickets and snacks for everyone) have become a once-in-a-while treat, not a routine occurrence. Now, we regularly test the "fun doesn't have to cost you" theory, and we play more board games at home and Frisbee golf in the park.

Twice-a-week Chinese takeout and/or pizza has become every other week, and instead we make turkey tacos in the Crock-Pot with Mexican soda pop, or Asian chicken and broccoli with store-bought fortune cookies. Ironically, the less we spend on family time, the closer we get. The Amish would not be surprised by this. They know investing in relationships is a far greater venture than devoting money for material things. Their pared-down lifestyle, slower in rhythm than ours but rich in togetherness, has produced a type of closeness that can't be bought.

> This is another great gift of the Amish way of wealth: they share what they have with neighbors, Plain and Fancy both, which has a wonderful, full-circle effect.

"The Amish are a 'people culture,'" said Erik Wesner. "Without television, and all the rest, much time is spent with friends and loved ones, and they've also got a lot of opportunities at hand to help one another out." This is another great gift of the Amish way of wealth: they share what they have with neighbors, Plain and Fancy both, which has a wonderful, full-circle effect.

Last summer, during our Period of Extreme Thrift, this got me thinking. *What can we share?* I wondered.

My husband, the Fish Slayer himself, had the answer. Our freezer was full of gorgeous, yummy salmon, caught recently in the waters of Lake Michigan. We gifted our new neighbors with several fillets, and they were thrilled. Doyle likes to say that when you give people salmon fillets, they behave as if you just gave them a bag of twenty-dollar bills. In return, they brought cookies and casseroles. The chef a couple of doors down presented us with frozen bags of his sumptuous meaty marinara sauce. Giving and receiving these humble edible gifts felt like a million bucks.

"Sharing with others is the brotherly love way of looking at a dollar," said Bishop Jake. "We loan our binder or machinery to someone else who doesn't have one, or our horses. We visit the sick, and we help bring in the harvest for those who can't. If you didn't help your neighbor, there would be something wrong."

Can't Buy Me Love

George, Paul, Ringo, and John knew it, and so do the Amish: money can't buy happiness. Smarter, slower money

※ ※ ※

habits can, however, pay off in big dividends. Since I meta-phorically hopped in an Amish buggy a little less than a year ago, on a quest to find out what this fascinating culture could teach me about money, the rewards have been manifold.

I learned to pay attention and be mindful of money, to make do with what I already had, and to outsmart my desires and improve my self-control. Flexing that once soft and floppy thrift muscle is now automatic instead of something I have to struggle to do. I've discovered how to cut back without feeling deprived; in fact, I feel just the opposite, as if now, on the other side of this quirky Amish trip, I have an abundance of creativity, resourcefulness, and peace I didn't have before.

I've learned to measure spending against my life's goals and deepest desires, and I have the Amish to thank for it. Their timeless, simple rituals of saving, sharing, and shoofly pie have caused them to thrive for hundreds of years.

May they continue to thrive for hundreds more.

⌗ ⌗ ⌗

ACKNOWLEDGMENTS

My abiding thanks to the following folks, whose time, wisdom, expertise, and hospitality enhanced this book immeasurably:

To Amish friends in Lancaster County, Pennsylvania, and Muskegon and Macomb Counties in Michigan, my sincere thanks for opening your doors to an outsider and trusting me with your privacy and wonderful money wisdom. I will never forget your gentle helpfulness.

Bill O'Brien: I couldn't have done this without you, Bill, and I thank you. Your sense of humor came shining through that first phone interview, and I knew this would be a fun book. Thanks especially to you and your wife for inviting me to dinner that awful day in February!

Erik Wesner: Your encouragement and insight into the Amish community enriched this book. Thanks a million!

Dr. Donald Kraybill: Thank you for your kindness and for

※ ※ ※

taking the time to be interviewed. No one knows more about the Amish than you, and your comprehensive knowledge and sensitivity deepened this book considerably.

Diane Goslin: Thanks much for your kindness and hospitality to me, and for taking good care of me at your lovely cottage bed-and-breakfast, Laurel Inn the Hollow. Thanks for introducing me to some of your Amish friends as well, and for your wealth of wisdom on the Amish community.

Will and Dana Kenny: For your long-term friendship and for being impeccable—and fun—hosts to my family while we were in Harrisburg, my sincere thanks and love.

Thanks to Hope Adair from Breton Travel for her tenacious help.

Also, thanks to Devon Hamstra, Russ and Linda Johnson, and others who helped me connect with those in the Amish community.

To Tracy Bianchi, author of *Green Mama*, for the fantastic tips on recycling and reusing!

I owe a debt of gratitude to my friends at Thomas Nelson, including Jennifer Womble and Brenda Smotherman, who have been a pleasure to work with over the last few years on various projects. Many thanks to Joel Miller, who went to the mat for this book, and who got the idea instantly. Thanks for being such an encouragement to me and my writing. And to Bryan Norman, an editor and friend, thanks for being an unexpected blessing to me.

To my incomparable agent, Esther Fedorkevitch, whom I

⌘ ⌘ ⌘

adore and who fought for this book every step of the way, my fervent thanks and much love.

Thanks to Ken and Linda Craker, who took my kids more than once, and even took Phoebe to Wyoming for a week, so I could finish this book on time. Love you. Also, thanks aplenty to my "bonus" mom and dad, George and Pat Vanderlaan, for support and love.

To my beautiful mom, Linda Reimer, who grew up "semi-Amish" in some ways, and who always prays and always supports me, whatever I am doing!

I could not be the writer and woman I aim to be without the never-ending, soul-filling wisdom and cheerleading of my Sisterhood of the Traveling Nightie, aka The (Writers) Guild: Ann Byle, Shelly Beach, Tracy Groot, Angela Blyker, Cynthia Beach, Alison Hodgson, and Sharon Carrns. Thanks to Rhoda Janzen and Julie Barnhill for more writer-ly boosts here and there.

Last but not least, all my love and devotion to my husband, Doyle, and my children, Jonah, Ezra, and Phoebe, for loving me and supporting me through it all, and for entering into the Amish Zone with me for quite some time!

✖ ✖ ✖

ABOUT THE AUTHOR

L orilee Craker is the author of eleven books, including
the *New York Times* best seller *Through the Storm* with
Lynne Spears. When not shuttling her three children to
hockey, gymnastics, and everywhere in between, Lorilee moon-
lights as an entertainment and features writer for the *Grand
Rapids Press* in Grand Rapids, Michigan, and has written for
magazines such as *Parents* and *Parent and Child*.